THE SOCIAL
ENTREPRENEURSHIP
OF
CHANGE

The Social Entrepreneurship of Change

Leonard J. Duhl, M.D.

Cogent Publishing
Putnam Valley, NY

Cogent Publishing
3 Miller Road
Putnam Valley, NY 10579

This Second Edition published by Cogent Publishing,
a division of The Whitson Group, Inc., 3 Miller Road, Putnam Valley, NY 10579.

Cogent Publishing books are available at special quantity discounts to use as premiums and sales promotions, or for use in corporate training programs. For more information please write the publisher.

Manufactured in the United States of America

Library of Congress Cataloging-in-Publication Data is available on request

ISBN 0-925776-04-1
10 9 8 7 6 5 4 3 2 1

BK
$ 11.69

Contents

Acknowledgements

This book has taken many years to complete. It is a product of a lifetime of concerns with health, planning policy and change. I focus both on the individual and the larger environment reflecting my preoccupation with the whole.

Personal and social change are my lifelong preoccupations. It came in large part from my father. He was interested in all that existed, and turned me on to the city, to nature and almost everything that I can think of. He taught me to question even the most accepted of apparent truths. He always wanted to change things for the better. My mother, on the other hand, brought love, warmth, caring and psychological support. These are central to change for the better.

While becoming a professional, Ed Greenwood and his wife Joan mentored me over the years of training in psychiatry and beyond. "You're doing great!" was what he often said. He introduced me to more and more people in and around psychiatry and the community. His friend and mine, Karl Menninger, now in his ninety-sixth year young, is a model of a passionate and inquisitive therapist and citizen. He encouraged me to be a continuous spark for change.

There have been many more in my life who supported and encouraged me. The founding Director of the National Institute of Mental Health, Robert Felix, is the most unique of leaders. He stimulated, sustained and expanded my responsibility. His vision made the NIMH a key player for social change. I consider him a model social entrepreneur. He said to me, "Go out and talk for the Institute. In public, I will support you right or wrong. If, however, you create problems, I will deal with you privately!'' He never did. I grew at NIMH, and I thank him profusely.

Then there are the friends, Bill Soskin, Erich Lindemann and Rosalind Lindheim (all now deceased), John Seeley, Dick Smith, Sheldon Margen, Varindra Tarzie Vittachi, Hal Visotsky, Robert Aldrich, Don Schon, Warren Bennis, Barney and Bernice Weissbourd, Carl Eisdorfer, Ian Grand, Art Kohrman, Jack Rosenthal, Peter Fillipelli, Martyn Webb, Dick Boone, Howell Baum, Richard Perl, Steve Blum, Nestor Gonzales, Trevor Hancock, Mayer Spivack, Ben Snyder, and so many more. In almost all instances their families, as well as mine, play a big role in my life.

I could go on and on with the list of those who make up the "floating crap game" of family and friends. Many are part of the old Space Cadets, a group that met for eleven years while I was at NIMH, and explored new ways of thinking about humans and their environment. All are deeply committed to strong personal and social values, in their continued involvement in change for the common good.

In addition there is my brother Fred. His interests in family therapy, using similar concepts, encouraged me in many ways. All my children, Pamela, Nina, David, Susan and Aurora, through their education of me, and our continual interaction have shown that I may be on the right course. Thanks to all five and their families.

The book itself is a joint creation with Erna Olafson. My being a dyslexic, even with the new found friend a computer, makes writing difficult. She with her background in history and an emerging interest in family therapy, did the major work of making me intelligible. Without her, this book would not have been produced.

John Steiner and Mischa Taubman, both friends, supported Erna's work financially, while we wrote it. Bill Whitson, another good friend, started this book on the way to a publisher. Ivor Whitson worked with the publisher, Pace University Press, to bring all the work to fruition.

I thank them all, including the unnamed friends, my former wife, Carola (now, sadly, deceased), and my father-in-law Robert Meyer, who have participated in, nurtured and supported my personal and social search.

My wife Lisa has had to live with the archeological layers of my mind as well as the many things I seem to get into. She sometimes edits, often questions and continually sustains my interests in innumerable ways.

Len Duhl
Berkeley, California
May 1, 1989

Preface 2000

The Social Entrepreneurship of Change has remained current since its appearance in 1993. In looking at what has occurred within these last years, what some saw as inconsequential or irrelevant has become *"the only way to go."* Society has become even more complex. World trends increasingly affect local communities. NAFTA, the World Trade Organization and the International Monetary Fund's policies of *"structural readjustment"* are some of the international economic forces that have lead to an emergence of activities on the community level everywhere in the world.

Wherever I visit, I find a new kind of entrepreneur. These social entrepreneurs are using their skills, not for profit and gain, but to increase the quality of life of their communities. Many of them are women. They are organizing with zeal previously unknown. The Internet and email have increased their ability to obtain information, to communicate with others and to organize. They find themselves in leadership roles in community initiatives to solve community problems.

Since there is little money for grass roots' initiatives, communities have had to find other resources. These resources include the people, voluntary organizations, churches, and the business community. Communities seek to find a *common ground*, a mutually beneficial situation to deal with environmental and social problems, and with the needs of their worker-families and their organizations. They find that what money they need can be found locally through local contacts. Ever more, they are bringing together individuals and groups with a common interest and those whose actions impinge on their concerns.

Each community develops its own priorities. These may be building or redesigning a school, dealing with pollution, housing, parks, transportation, jobs or crime. To deal with these issues, entrepreneurs and their allies must find resources besides money on which they can call. What are the assets of communities?

Often, the act of organizing and communication is enough to make change.

The attempt of Oakland California to deal with a very high infant mortality rate in impoverished neighborhoods, is a case in point. The infant mortality rate had been high for many years. Every attempt to intervene using the best public health programs has failed. People were frustrated, discouraged and despairing.

A *social entrepreneur*, Angela Blackwell, and her team called together everyone concerned with the high infant mortality rate to form a coalition. Simultaneously, she organized other coalitions on education, jobs, transportation, housing, health, welfare and more.

A Coalition of Coalitions brought together all these groups, to discuss the high infant mortality rate. Several wanted to leave but were persuaded to remain. At the end of six months of discussions, *without* any new programs, or increased spending, the infant mortality rate dropped 50 percent, and has remained down. For the first time the total community mobilized its assets in a systemic way, connecting through relationships, and finding a new way to work with clients.

What then makes a *social entrepreneur?* In the book I attempt to show how potential entrepreneurs, who may never before have worked in their community, can become catalysts for their communities. Most often, they are guided by long held values of concern for others. They are the people who care, based on their values and often on their spiritual beliefs. They come from every corner of the community, every social class and interest. Being unaware of their potential, *mentors* are necessary to start them on their way.

The question of the values that lie behind community decision making is important. Spirituality, the meaning of our lives, appears to be a key motivator of social entrepreneurial action, and community activity. Whether as a part of organized religion or not, spiritual values guide us in an age of profit and *the bottom line*. It is interesting that so often in our history we have used money as a replacement for personal concern. Using money as the common denominator has resulted in the power of special interests, competition, fragmentation, and a loss of a common identity—the community. We are a diverse, heterogeneous society, that must teach itself to embrace difference and to work for the *common good*.

In the program of Healthy Cities and Communities, we have shown the process of how it can be done. Since 1993, the number of these cities and communities worldwide has grown to more than seventy-five hundred. Most important is the increasing awareness that *"everything is connected"* and thus a broad systemic and ecological participatory approach is necessary. As one looks at other endeavors such as *Safe Cities, Livable Cities, Ecological Cities, Cold Cities,* and *Sustainable Cities,* we see this approach spreading.

There are many examples, one is the work of Steven Bingler, who helps communities use their total community and their resources as a school. Working with teachers, parents, students and the broader population, he has created a new kind of school out of museums and farms, and has turned cities into educating communities. Examples abound of these and other community endeavors that can be found on the Internet. Let me recommend two sites: www.healthycities.org and www.healthycommunities.org. Each can direct you to the Community Tool Box (http://ctb.lsi.ukans.edu/), a magnificent place for entrepreneurs to find help. There are many more.

The multiplying of resources for the social entrepreneur is impressive. I hope that these developments will continue to increase the quality of life of our diverse communities and their people. I see diversity as a blessing, bringing new ideas, and ways of living to communities. We must learn the "governance of diversity." We can only do so, as we struggle, issue by issue, locally to find ways of finding a mutually beneficial solution for the *common good*. These actions will encourage more to call upon their altruistic values, find allies, and begin the processes of increasing the quality of life for all.

LEONARD J. DUHL
BERKELEY, CALIFORNIA
JANUARY 9, 2000

Preface

> We are living in the time of the Parenthesis, the time between eras. . . .
> Although the time between eras is uncertain, it is a great and yeasty time,
> filled with opportunity. If we can learn to make uncertainty our friend,
> we can achieve more than in stable eras. In stable eras, everything has a
> name and everything knows its place, and we can leverage very little.
>
> But in the time of the Parenthesis, we have extraordinary leverage and
> influence—individually, professionally, and institutionally—if we can
> only get a clear sense, a clear conception, a clear vision, of the road
> ahead. (Naisbitt)

I have borrowed Naisbitt's idea of the parenthesis to describe the
disturbing times we are traversing because it evokes images of an
opening and a space between categories. The parenthesis is a neutral
image, and in its pause there are limitless possibilities for change,
trouble, or peace. Naisbitt, a relatively optimistic futurist, ends the
passage cited above by exclaiming, "My God, what a fantastic time to
be alive!"

John Naisbitt is not alone, although he is cheerier than most. Others
have begun to publish projections for the future that offer some hope,
first of all that there can *be* a human future, and secondly, that human
choice may play some role in shaping it. Paul Hawken, James Ogilvy,
and Peter Schwartz of the Stanford Research Institute are among such
futurists, and their *Seven Tomorrows* offers a variety of possible
scenarios for the eighties and nineties. They begin this work by
asserting, "The future is unsettled, yet we need a future we can believe

in." What does it mean to say that we need a possible future? As Hawken and his coauthors explain it, "Prospects of doom paralyze action just as certainly as naive hopes render action unnecessary. A society deprived of all hope suffers a kind of morbidity." The aim of *Seven Tomorrows* is "to project alternative futures so that responsible and intelligent choice is possible." The authors conclude that, "We need a future we can affirm, a future that is neither so hopeful as to be unrealistic, nor so grim as to invite despair. Optimism and pessimism are not arguments. They are opposite forms of the same surrender to simplicity. . . ."

If, indeed, prospects of doom paralyze action, we all have reason to despair, for gloomy prognostications have become so commonplace as to numb us. Here, for example, is Gerald Durrell on the environmental crisis.

> At the present rate of 'progress,' and unless something is done quickly, disaster stares us in the face. Erosion, desertification and pollution have become our lot. It is a weird form of suicide, for we are bleeding our planet to death. We are led by sabre-rattling politicians who are ignorant of biology, beset by sectarian groups noted for their narrow-mindedness and intolerance, surrounded by powerful commercial interests whose only interest in nature is often to rape it. We are misguided and misled, trotting to oblivion as obediently as the Gadarene Swine. I wonder what the attitude will be if, in a hundred years' time, this book is read by our starving grandchildren—and they see that this decimation of their inheritance was recognized, cures for it were available, and nothing was done?
>
> Make no mistake about it, a cure is possible. (in Myers)

Even with the final exhortation, this is a discouraging vision.

And here is a sample from Fritjof Capra's generally positive *Turning Point* that focuses on nuclear holocaust.

> At the beginning of the last two decades of our century, we find ourselves in a state of profound, world-wide crisis. It is a complex, multi-dimensional crisis whose facets touch every aspect of our lives—our health and livelihood, the quality of our environment and our social relationships, our economy, technology, and politics. It is a crisis of intellectual, moral and spiritual dimensions; a crisis on a scale and urgency unprecedented in recorded human history. For the first time we have to face the very real threat of extinction of the human race and of all life on this planet.

From another futurist, Medard Gabriel, we have a diagnosis and cure that stresses interconnection and the need for global planning.

Society, from local communities to the global commonwealth, has problems. This is nothing new. What is new is the unparalleled complexity, interconnectedness, and danger inherent in these problems as a result of their global scope, as well as the destructive power of today's weapons
. . .

Unfortunately, there is nothing in the world today that could pass for "global planning"—unless you count what some elements of the military and multinational corporations are doing. And, in those cases, what is happening is not addressing the major needs of humanity for food, energy, health care, shelter, education, and employment, but rather the special-interest needs (or demands) of a select few. It's "global planning" not for the globe but for the few.

And finally, Dr. Alice Miller, a Swiss psychotherapist whose sensitive revision of classical psychoanalytic theory has been well received in the United States, points to the poisonous pedagogy of our child raising practices as the origin of human destructiveness. She writes:

It requires no great effort to identify the apocalyptic features of our century: world wars, massacres, the specter of nuclear war, the enslavement of millions by technology and totalitarian regimes, the threat to the earth's ecological balance, the depletion of energy sources, the increase in drug addiction—the list could go on and on. Yet the same century has also brought us knowledge that is utterly new in human history and that could bring about a decisive change in our lives if its full significance were to penetrate public consciousness. I am referring to the discovery that the period of early childhood is of crucial importance for a person's emotional development. The more distinctly we come to see that the most ominous events of the present and recent past are not the products of mature rationality and the more clearly we recognize the absurdity and unpredictability of the arms race, the more urgent becomes the need to investigate the origins and nature of the human destructiveness whose helpless victims we all are. The magnitude of destructiveness that we read about in newspapers every day actually represents only the last chapter of long stories we are usually ignorant of. We are victims, observers, reporters, or mute witnesses of a violence whose roots we do not see.

I.

Setting the Stage

We are living in the midst of all-encompassing world-wide social and political change, where many people and communities challenge, resist, and modify inherited ways of living. Questioning and defiance of authority occur everywhere from family to school to workplace, and bizarre revivals of primitive patterns of hierarchy emerge in response to this disintegration. Institutions and individuals are finding that they can no longer respond effectively to problems as they emerge. Our fragmented institutions, each going their own ways—in the family, the economy, the government, or in world-wide society—are finding that existing patterns of governance, that is, ways to be part of a whole, no longer work, and that new forms of organization must be found.

A great many people in all parts of the world have expressed the fear that no public or political solution can be found for these assorted problems of tyranny, fragmentation, polarization, narcissism, violence and institutional disarray. As one observer of the contemporary American scene summarizes his view of the present, "It's amazingly simple. Things fall apart. There's nothing you can do. Let a smile be your umbrella." (Hougan).

Models of government or business where leaders such as patriarchs, corporate presidents, boards of directors, or governors control and rule now seem to function badly or not at all. Governments and public agencies throughout the United States—and, indeed, around the world—are confronting unprecedented problems in the 1980s. In some cases, as in the radical right in America or in Khomeni's Iran, masses of people seek order and certainty in repressive political and social

1

forms that blend religion and politics and blur the distinction between public and private. Such nostalgic retreats to simpler forms and simpler times, to patriarchy, hierarchy, and religion provoke yet another old response, that of violent terrorist or revolutionary activity to transform government and society. These nineteenth-century alternatives of hierarchy or revolution are as antique as buggies and landaus; they impede creative thinking as we speed toward the twenty-first century.

The current crisis is intensified by the erosion of the confident positivist assumptions of an earlier generation of social scientists and social activists who have seen unintended consequences and unforeseen events swamp even the best of their programs. In the United States years of rising costs and repeated rounds of funds cutbacks have left many public agencies virtually impotent. In addition, the erosion of institutional authority and structure on many levels of social organization, from the family to the White House, points to a deep, persistent malaise that seems to have no remedy.

An alarming number of those with the authority and training to effect change no longer have the conviction that human crises can be met with positive action and that social problems can be grasped and solved. As inherited models of social change have shown themselves inadequate to meet the current crises, many of those in power have succumbed to the apathy most often associated with poverty and powerlessness. They seem unable to envision the future or indeed to act in ways that accomplish more than to relieve the shrillest pains or to satisfy personal, shortsighted ambitions without thought for a wider context. Even the best popular press now celebrates successful salespeople and investors—men and women whose sole achievement has been to make a good deal of money—in their profiles of success and as models for the young. No wider vision seems possible. Temporal projections and spatial connections have constricted to a tight, bounded present.

Fritjof Capra (1982) assesses this intellectual impoverishment as follows:

> It is a striking sign of our time that the people who are supposed to be experts in various fields can no longer deal with the urgent problems that have arisen in their areas of expertise. . . . None of them, however, identified the real problem that underlies the crisis of ideas: the fact that most academics subscribe to narrow perceptions of reality which are inadequate for dealing with the major problems of our time. These problems, as we shall see in detail, are systemic problems, which means

that they are closely interconnected and interdependent. They cannot be understood within the fragmented methodology characteristic of our academic disciplines and government agencies. . . . A resolution can be found only if the structure of the web itself is changed, and this will involve profound transformations of our social institutions, values, and ideas. As we examine the sources of our cultural crisis, it will become apparent that most of our leading thinkers use outdated conceptual models and irrelevant variables.

This book arises from the conviction that politicians, planners, community groups, and other public advocates can and must adapt themselves to meet the contemporary crisis. I believe that the "profound transformations" in ideas and institutions Capra describes are possible, and I suggest a number of ways in which such adaptation or transformation might occur and offer examples of successful transitions to new models of planning on the many levels and on varied scales from local to global. The planning method and style described here could be applied on the local or international level, in business as well as in community or public affairs.

If the time in which we live is indeed the crisis many futurists say it is, it has also become something of a commonplace in certain circles to note that the Chinese characters for crisis, *wei-ji,* are two, the first meaning "danger" and the second, "opportunity." One sees this translation not only in serious works, such as Capra's *Turning Point* (p.26), but seemingly everywhere, on wall posters, greeting cards, and in newspaper articles. Perhaps the news that needs to get around is that there is opportunity in this crisis and that we need not retire to the Wailing Wall. It may be premature to undertake our preparatory mourning for human civilization. Annihilation is not certain.

The evidence is overwhelming that planning as it was once understood no longer works, but the response to this need not be cultural collapse. We are not an isolated society faced with the destruction of our ancient totems. We possess both the mental agility and the institutional flexibility to rethink the entire process of social change and planning for the future. We have the ability to look at our conceptual frameworks and institutional structures from the outside and to shake and shuffle and reconstruct them to meet the needs of the 1990s and beyond. The received wisdom of the social and political sciences is not written in stone. What is needed now is systems planning on a global scale. Nothing less will do.

This is not a book of social plans. It is not even primarily about how to plan and carry through proposals. It is, instead, a book about how to *think* about planning creatively in new ways which overcome the paralysis inflicted on us by our present largely defunct cognitive and institutional structures.

This new way of thinking about change involves a profound reconditioning of our entire attitude toward the environment. If the needs of past millenia have conditioned us to master an alien and often hostile environment and to compete with others for control and ownership of what we have appropriated, can we now alter that conditioning and thereby regain access to the multiple other possibilities for vision and action inherent in our natures? That question becomes urgent as a Western model of control and a single-track, Western model of "development" spreads around the world, extinguishing what remains in other cultures of alternative possibilities for human behavior. These other models, which are in many cases non-hierarchical, non-competitive, and respectful of the "delicate fabric of living situations," may carry an ecological message we need as the West finally learns that the earth is one, finite, and interconnected. It may even be argued that part of the contemporary crisis of confidence in the West derives from the challenge to Western value systems posed by these alternative visions.

Western science, however, has led us to the same point. We have reached the limits of the Baconian and Cartesian imperative to "make ourselves the masters and possessors of nature." As Gerald Durrell has said, our long struggle to dominate nature has reached the point where we are bleeding the planet to death. But, if She dies, we die. Many Native American, African and Asian spiritual traditions taught—and in rare cases still teach—that the Earth is a Mother to be nourished, celebrated, and respected. They have been wiser than we, for they knew what we are just learning, that a child cannot survive without its parent. Ecologically, these "primitives" were more successful than we, and they disturbed the ecosystem far less. It is not their belief systems and practices that have brought us to our present pass.

As Capra and others have pointed out, our thinking in the West has been distorted by mechanistic thinking and its misguided application to the complex and interconnected world of living organisms. Capra (1982) writes:

> In classical science nature was seen as a mechanical system composed on basic building blocks. In accordance with this view, Darwin proposed

a theory of evolution in which the unit of survival was the species, the subspecies, or some other building block of the biological world. But a century later it has become quite clear that the unit of survival is not any of these entities. What survives is the organism-in-its-environment. An organism that thinks only in terms of its own survival will invariably destroy its environment and, as we are learning from bitter experience, will thus destroy itself. (288–89)

Even if we do wound the earth and destroy ourselves, our planet may recover. It may take a million years, but this is not long in a lifespan of billions. It is we who will be gone.

If, then, this human organism is to survive in this environment, we must give up our desire to master, dominate and *control* nature. Does it, however, make any sense to talk about planning for the future in a context of non-control? For one of the sources of contemporary despair and apathy is the often voiced perception that everything—from childrearing to international monetary systems—has gone out of control. Systems cannot be ruled and manipulated in ways that once seemed possible, nor can plans be imposed on the stuff of human society. Can one make an ally of the uncontrollable and still preserve fundamental human values? What exactly do we mean by non-control? Futurists Paul Hawken and others at the Stanford Research Institute offer this partial answer:

We would argue that no one is in control of the current course of history, not the President of the United States, not bankers like David Rockefeller, not "the international communist conspiracy." Nor is our fate totally determined by the inexorable dwindling of our resources or by other material and economic forces. Instead, humanity stands at a unique point: simultaneously our problems are so acute and our communication network so widespread that, for the first time in world history, genuinely collective and democratic decisions are both demanded and possible. In order to choose intelligently, we need a sufficiently widespread consciousness of our condition and of our capacity to alter it through the decisions of enough people. We need a collective intelligence of a kind that may not have characterized the human species in the past; but we see no reason to believe that, given the highly developed nervous system of an advanced communications network, a whole population cannot reach a stage of mature self-consciousness much as an individual does. (p.9)

If no one is in control, no one is to blame, and we confront chaos. I suspect that the proliferation of conspiracy theories in the last generation reflects the wish to believe that *someone*—even the enemy, the multinationals, the Communists, the CIA, whoever—is in control. If some group has power, power can be seized. Most of us would rather confront conspiracy than chaos.

To liberate the "collective intelligence" of which Hawken and company speak, planning can no longer be left only to the expert professionals, the men in charge. Non-control planning means that the professionals to whom this book is addressed (among others) have to let go of the ways they have been taught to think, to act, and to see themselves. None of this is easy, but the toughest part of it may be the abandonment of cherished professional self-images of power and competence. The new self-imagery may be that of the gardener or the midwife instead of the engineer. And it may help to note that non-control planning harkens back to venerable traditions of participatory democracy. As Medard Gabriel puts it:

> Planning needs to be viewed as something done *by* society, not *for* society. Planners need to view themselves as facilitators of social decision-making. Their job should be to make explicit the alternatives facing their constituents, to supply the information needed to make rational decisions, and to encourage others to take part in decision-making. The planners' success should be judged by the number of people they involve in the planning process, not by how secretive they can be. (p.22)

Here we come to the core of our crisis and perhaps the key leverage point for change. However fragmented institutions may be and however badly systems may be working, it remains true that some sort of power—over the earth's resources, over production, over weaponry, over our common fate—is concentrated in the hands of relatively few men (and they are almost all men) in governments and industries around the world. There is nothing in history, at least not in Western history, that would suggest that men voluntarily surrender such power. The possibility that there will be violent struggle—a world-wide cataclysm—to bring down these men is very real, a possible dark chapter ahead. I would simply argue, with Hawken and others, that these are not the only possible tomorrows, that we do not have to choose between violent revolution on the one hand or passive acceptance on the other while men bleed the planet to death. Our current danger and interconnection is so great that in either case the perpetrators will become victims. Can elites transform themselves and voluntarily share power when their survival, along with the lives of all the rest of us, depends on their doing so? Maybe. We have never been in such a situation before. I believe, with Hawken, that it is not impossible for humans to reach a "collective intelligence of a kind that may not have characterized the human species in the past." Old enemies may meet there. Richard Nixon did go to China. Nothing human is constant except change.

We cannot, then, solve our current problems with "outdated conceptual models and irrelevant variables," nor will old, hierarchical patterns of planning and governance work. Systems thinking on a global scale, participatory planning, paths that abandon quixotic illusions of control, all would seem to be the order of the day. As with all major conceptual shifts, learning these new ways may create profound unease. Paradoxically, however, recognizing the limits of what we can achieve may free us to act in the limited field available. As Hawken and colleagues point out, optimism and despair are simply two faces of a surrender to simple-minded thinking.

Our dilemma is not new. Paradigm shifts have occurred again and again in our history. When Moses led the Jews out of Egypt, he and his followers spent 40 years in the desert. The modern Israelis have proven in a number of recent wars that the Sinai is easily crossed, and even for the primitive transport of Moses' time, 40 years of travel seems outlandish. Why did Moses and his followers take so long to cross this modest desert? It seems that the personal and social transitions from the fleshpots of Egypt to freedom in the Promised Land required a change of perceptions, and the human mind is not easily transformed. It was essential to give up the slave-like ways that had been learned in Egypt. By the time the Jews reached their homeland, all but two persons who remembered Egypt had died off, so that new people, readied in the desert for the Promised Land, completed the journey and entered upon their inheritance reborn. In the emptiness of the desert, in this pause, transformation could occur.

The time in the desert was 40 years, "The Time of the Parenthesis," when skins are shed, fish breathe, and worms fly. In human terms, mind and culture shift profoundly at such times. The changes during such periods, and they have occurred many times in world history, are often not clearly understood. Forty represents an ancient healing interval as well. For example, the Venetians, exposed to the Black Plague, ordered a quarantine (*quarantino* or 40) of 40 days to allow the disease to die out, and to build up the healthy resistance of the population. The Venetians did not understand the germ theory of disease, and the healing space of 40 days was almost certainly religious in origin; Jesus, after all, spent 40 days in the desert before beginning to teach. What the Venetians did understand was that time permitted processes to unfold. I hold no brief for 40 as a magical number, nor for the religious significance of the interval. What I do believe is that change involves a death and rebirth and that time unfolds in rich and surprising ways. Old habits of thought can suffocate this growth. Seeds do not thrive in crowded gardens.

This, then, is a "how-to" book with the choice of its ending left up to all of us as participants. At the risk of sounding naive, I have set out to write a moderately hopeful book, a book about change that envisions a human future. I am writing near the end of the most brutal century in recorded history, while torture, war, terrorism, tyranny, over-population, starvation, and environmental catastrophes affect or threaten us like the seven ancient plagues. Perhaps because our situation is so desperate, the positive imagery of choice and of time ahead can act as a saving leap of faith. To Immanuel Kant's categorical imperatives of God, freedom, and immortality we would add new words for our time—choice, and a possible future.

The Kalahari pygmies have a saying that there is a dream dreaming us. Our human images, however, can be tyrants. If we let annihilation, holocaust, or Armageddon be the images that guide us—as they were for Hitler, with his demented dreams of victory or Götterdammerung— then we invite the very obliteration we dread. Plans made and actions taken with the belief that life on earth will be violently destroyed within a generation will be ruled by that hopeless image. Polls show that an alarming number of young people believe that such destruction is inevitable, while our elderly President Reagan revealed that he is preoccupied with images of ours as the age of Armageddon. To have any hope for human survival, we must shift the images of death and destruction from their central place in our consciousness, for research on the impact of labelling suggests that images shape individual behavior powerfully. The scapegoated child becomes bad. The identified schizophrenic learns to act mad. So too, I suggest, for collective experience. A human race that believes it is drifting fatally and inevitably towards the destruction of life will destroy life. The challenge is to retain some hope while not looking away from human cruelty, ignorance, and greed.

Many spiritual and healing traditions use visualization in order to heal, and the images visualized range from wrathful to serene. To heal ourselves means to contact this wholeness, this *holiness,* and to visualize human futures that embrace all of what we are and can be, the light, the dark, and all the other shades. It is possible that human nature and human possibilities are far more complex than most ideologies and philosophies assert and that we may have untapped capacities to come through this time of danger and opportunity. The dream that dreams us may be richer than we know.

What follows does not merely express a wish that things turn out all right. Throughout the world there are a variety of movements and endeavors that are quietly exploring new paths. Many of these experiments are hidden, because, as an editor of *The New York Times* once remarked, "They are not news." The hunger for a new spirituality reaches the newspapers only in exposés of the shoddiest and most repressive of cults. The search for community is discredited by the horror at Jonestown. Corporate experiments in participatory management fare somewhat better, but they often receive a critical press.

Meanwhile, the quiet successes, the green grass of change, go on virtually unnoticed. I will be describing some such movements in the pages that follow. Many are in process, emergent and fragile, while others are mature and proven, although mostly ignored by the world's media.

I tell stories about this creative ferment in chapters that explicitly set out the values and principles that guide me as well as in the how-to sections for map making and planning entrepreneurship. Throughout the book, health is a central metaphor, because of its spaciousness as an idea, because it is ideologically neutral, and because of the linguistic roots that Kierkegaard once noted that health shares with *whole* and *holy*. I will have more to say about these connections in what follows; here I wish to point out that I have chapters both about health and social change, and about the healthy city or *polis*, the local arena where change proceeds.

The book is an *essay*, a beginning, my best attempt for now. I hope you understand what I am trying to say.

* * * * * *

Pauline epistle   1 Corinthians 13

If I speak in the tongues of men and of angels but have not love, I am a noisy gong or a clanging cymbal.
And if I have prophetic powers and understand all mysteries and all knowledge
And if I have all faith in all its fullness so as to move mountains but have not love I am nothing.
If I give away all I have
If I deliver my body to be burned but have not love, I gain nothing.

Love is patient and kind.
Love is not jealous or boastful. It is not arrogant or rude.
Love does not insist on its own way. It is not irritable or resentful.
It does not rejoice at wrong but rejoices in the right.
Love bears all things, believes all things, hopes all things, endures all things.
Love never ends.
As for prophecies, they will pass away
As for tongues, they will cease
As for knowledge, it will pass away
For our knowledge is imperfect and our prophecies imperfect
But when the perfect comes the imperfect will pass away.
When I was a child I spoke like a child, I thought like a child, I reasoned like a child
But when I became an adult I gave up childish ways
For now we see in a mirror dimly
But then face to face
Now I know in part
Then I shall understand fully even as I have been fully understood.
So faith, hope, and love abide, these three
But the greatest of these is love.

* * * * * *

It was a long time before I could finally take seriously the doubts about the drive theory that had kept troubling me ever since the days of my training as an analyst and could finally stop feeling obligated to regard it as the cornerstone of psychoanalysis, but I had to take this step if I was to remain loyal to my basic principle of learning from my patients instead of trying to make them fit my theories.

Alice Miller
Thou Shalt Not Be Aware, p. 121

* * * * * *

It may be that when we no longer know what to do we have come to our real work and that when we no longer know which way to go we have begun our real journey. The mind that is not baffled is not employed. The impeded stream is the one that sings.

Wendell Barry
"Poetry and Marriage"

II.

Values

The fundamental question I ask is this: can one, given the contemporary world-wide crisis, still talk about values and planning in a way that has any meaning? We have seen old models of social change become defunct and even new institutions become outmoded before they are fully formed, like nails in rainy climates that rust before use on construction sites. Inherited patterns of authority and leadership are everywhere challenged. Change has become so rapid that crisis builds on crisis, and we seem to live in a permanent state of emergency. An ever-increasing planetary interdependence allows no refuge from disorders wherever they may break out. The gap between the rich nations and the poor nations continues to widen, and many who live in prosperity have withdrawn into a lifeboat mentality. Given all this, can one think about and try to plan for the future in ways that foster certain fundamental moral principles? Is there some middle road between the somewhat naive optimism of our liberal past and the current atmosphere of selfishness, shortage, apathy, and crisis? Will change have to come violently?

The values of which I speak are nothing very novel. I remember an old "My Day" column by Eleanor Roosevelt in which she commented on the simplicity and antiquity of the greatest human ideas and noted that they are expressed in almost mundane words. The Puritans even named their children for these principles: Faith, Hope, Tolerance, and "the greatest of these," Charity—which also means Love. Ancient Buddhist teachings about Compassion refer not merely to kindly intentions carried out with effort but to a state of vigorous understanding about transience and interconnection from which beneficial action naturally flows. Dharmas, or rules of behavior, are found in all religions, even our own contemporary religion of Materialism.

The human services agencies at the United Nations have voiced the principles to which I refer many times. Their familiarity, however, makes them no less precious. For individuals, they entail the right to full growth and development and the provision of food, clothing, shelter, and education. Health is a goal as well—not the mere absence of sickness, but health as wholeness, flexibility and fullness. The principles of human rights also include personal freedom and some control over the events that affect one's life. On the group and community level, these values favor creating ways for people to work together without exploitation, and finding a glue of trust, cooperation, and respect, so that communities may be formed that do minimal violence to individuals. On the global level, we are concerned with fair distribution of the earth's resources, an ecological awareness of the limitations and fragility of our planet, and the absence of violence between peoples. On every scale plunder, oppression, and exploitation violate these fundamental principles. There should be no rape of the earth and sea and air, no rape of communities, no rape of individuals.

Values are integral to the human sciences, to planning, and to any intervention for change. We all act according to certain standards of truth and of right and wrong, whether or not we are conscious of them *as* values. We are all located somewhere in the multiplicity of human cultures and world-views. The peculiarity, however, of the Western bourgeois civilization in which our social and political disciplines developed has been its universalizing tendency, its conviction that its version of reality—which includes subject/object duality, a lawful universe, the possibility of objective knowledge, linear time, and a solid, separate, observing self—was the *truth,* the way things really are. Built into this Western worldview has been a restless need to control and master the external environment. Seen as one value-system among many possibilities, this Western map, for all its successes in the technical and material realms, has aspects of arrogance, ethnocentrism, and spiritual emptiness. We are not the first to point out that the Promethean West has much to learn from the peoples it has conquered, from the more quiescent and communal cultures of the East and South. (David Landes, *The Unbound Prometheus*)

There are encouraging signs, indeed, that the old dichotomy between East and West may be breaking down in this new era of the global village. Creative—and often still quite small—movements around the world reveal a new community of beliefs and of re-emergent values that transcend the ancient differences and distinctions. It is impossible to see, at this point, how these similarities may develop in time and whether the actions they inspire will be strong enough to withstand the enormous momentum of the destructive forces of the late twentieth century, but these movements are hopeful signs amid the more frightening omens that surround us.

What are these hopeful signs in East and West and what does their congruence promise? Let us begin by examining the goals and sources of the Sarvodaya Movement in Sri Lanka and then compare its core values with those of small movements in the United States, the Communications Era Task Force located in Spokane, Washington, and several corporations.

The Sarvodaya Movement began in 1958 when a group of high school students from Nalanda College, a Buddhist high school in Colombo, Sri Lanka, went out into the impoverished villages of Sri Lanka on a two-week holiday work camp. These students were led by their science teacher, A.T. Ariyaratne, who wanted them "to understand and experience the true state of affairs that prevailed in the rural and poor urban areas . . . (and) to develop a love for their people and utilize the education they received to find ways of building a more just and happier life for them" (Joanna Macy, *Dharma and Development*, p. 24). Since this modest beginning, the Sarvodaya Movement has touched the lives of hundreds of thousands of villagers in Sri Lanka and has become internationally known both as an example and through the published works of Ariyaratne, who still leads this vast self-help endeavor.

In his writings, Ariyaratne has discussed the program's sources and goals according to six inter-related and mutually supportive categories. These categories are the social, the economic, the political, the moral, the cultural, and the spiritual.

His social teachings foster human equality and connection as well as the more traditional development goals of education and health. These social teachings strive to impart tolerance and compassion. Ariyaratne's social teachings are grounded in the Buddhist understanding of the "co-dependent arising" of all appearances. Westerners might understand codependent origination as describing the interconnection of man and nature, and of consciousness and matter. It means more than this, but at the least it means such an ecological or systems awareness. In all he writes Ariyaratne stresses the social example of

the Buddha as a teacher, healer, and reformer, so that he offers a
Buddhist parallel to the Christian social gospel.

Ariyaratne's economic program also mixes Western development
goals with the more classical values of the ancient Buddhist civilization
of Sri Lanka. The first goal is to produce goods so that people may
live, an urgent necessity in all "developing" countries. Secondly,
Ariyaratne states the need to conserve resources, that is to produce
only what is necessary and to inflict minimum damage on the ecosystem. Ariyaratne's third goal is to produce by cooperative methods
and his final one is to consume only what is "appropriate." These
economic objectives can be translated into the classical Buddhist
virtues of right livelihood and right effort, which are part of the
eightfold noble path.

The political aims of the movement are especially interesting to
Westerners in search of a new polity. These include decentralization
of power, widespread participation in decision-making, non-violence,
and freedom from coercion. These rules and practices are consistent
with those of the very earliest Buddhist *sanghas* (communities) and
with their teachings on non-violence, tolerance, and humility in the
face of things that cannot be controlled, but they are restated here in a
non-esoteric form that makes them accessible to the most secular of
Westerners.

The moral rules are simply a restatement of the five precepts of
Buddhism, and they are consistent with religious moral rules the world
over. These forbid killing, stealing, lying, sexual misconduct, and the
ingestion of harmful substances, which could include addictive drugs,
alcohol, or even violent television programs.

Culturally, the movement favors the recognition and nourishment of
cultural heterogeneity. Sarvodaya's cultural goals encourage harmony
in personal and physical relationships and the free expression in song,
dance, poetry and architecture of the indigenous spirit of each culture.
These cultural goals are consistent with the four principles of group
conduct common to Southern Buddhism, and with other teachings of
this ancient world-view, but again, they are restated here in modern
terms, and they have been tested in action in the movement.

As a planner, then, Ariyaratne is working on *trust;* he trusts that
those with whom he is working know what they need in terms of their
own values and culture, and he trusts that he can help release their
energies and confidence. Competence to shape one's own life is
health—and it is freedom. These are the ultimate values behind our
vision of planning. In the institutional ferment and chaos of the current

world, the planner can hope to stimulate others to create new forms that will meet their needs.

Planning entrepreneurs work in a non-hierarchical mode. They do not impose the values of their "superior" culture and technology on a benighted and ignorant people. They have learned to live in a world that is relative, complex, multivalent, uncertain, changing, and in many respects unknown. Not for them are the simplifications of a bi-polar world, right and wrong, God and the devil, Washington and Moscow. We repeat, however, that this non-control model of planning is easier to describe than to achieve. To be human is to be located, to have positions, ideas, values, a history, conscious and unconscious motives, and some wish to control things and to be right. The planning entrepreneur should, therefore, have at least two goals: to learn what one's own distorting lenses may be, both personal and cultural; and secondly, to have access to multiple other lenses, plans, or models of reality, so that one can work with others on their own terms.

The planner who stimulates others to action in this way teaches what he or she is learning. The Sarvodaya coordinators do not simply learn various skills, dig latrines, clean village wells, or build community centers. They are learning as well *how to learn,* how to change, and how to live and work with others in new ways. They are creating new institutional forms that are flexible, adaptable, and non-hierarchical. This approach is transforming rural Sri Lanka. Ariyaratne has said repeatedly, "A country cannot develop unless one has faith in the intelligence of the people." The Sarvodaya volunteers, who have touched the lives of people in an incredible 4,000 villages since the movement began in 1968, foster the intelligence, competence, confidence, and cooperativeness of villagers so that they can really help themselves. This is not just rhetoric; unlike the political infiltrators in Peruvian villages who talk self-help and impose their own brutal ideology by force and terror, the Sarvodaya movement really practices what it preaches.

In the first place, because it believes in local self reliance, Sarvodaya is organizationally decentralized. This radical and methodical decentralization took place when the movement was about 10 years old, and it involved a deliberate giving up of central control, including even control of money, the core of power in the modern world. Local village councils have legal status and have been incorporated with powers to develop their own programs of development. Not only is the structure as a whole non-hierarchical, but within each village, ancient hierarchies are upset; most councils contain equal and balanced numbers of men, women, and young people.

The Sarvodaya coordinator functions as a change entrepreneur. As one district coordinator put it, "The road we build may wash away, but the attitudes we build do not." (p. 54) Another Sarvodaya slogan goes, "We build the road and the road builds us." The work days that are known as *shramadanas* accomplish more than the task at hand, whether it be to build a well, school, road, or latrine.

The *process* is at least as important as the *product*. The common work experience, in which the Sarvodaya coordinator participates, does away with differences in status, differences between bureaucrat and villager, and social distinctions within the village. In this social learning experience, villagers learn to trust the outsider, and the outsider learns to respect the villagers. Everyone has a stake in what is built during the *shramadana*, so that villagers do not wait for outside experts to fix school roofs or clean out culverts. They have built these things, they have pride in them, and they feel competence and responsibility to keep them working.

Shramadanas have other festive, transformative ritual components. Food is shared. Many Sarvodaya organizers ask even impoverished villagers to contribute to this common meal, so that all will feel the power of giving and sharing. Working together and then eating together in celebration breaks down ancient village differences, statuses, and hierarchies; these activities soften boundaries that might keep villagers from cooperating in the future. These community meals also give villagers experience in organizing group events. Other activities that precede the actual work day include the planning sessions where ideas are shared, songs are sung, prayers recited, and dances performed.

It is from the people that change must come. Ariyaratne and his colleagues believe that the people themselves know best what they need. Outside experts, even if their technical skills are better, cannot really build what is needed. They cannot implant competence, confidence, intelligence, and community. Listening is, therefore, a skill in which all Sarvodaya organizers are trained—to be receptive, to hear, and to attend with respect, not with an assumed stance of respect, but with a genuine belief in the intelligence of the villagers. This is a long way from Marx's "idiocy of rural life" and is very different from European prejudices about the stupidity of the peasant. Almost every previous ideology that has come into the countryside has carried ideas developed in cities, in salons, in the British Museum reading room or in Parisian cafes. Sarvodaya ends this ancient colonization of the countryside by the town. It is really novel in *trusting* the intelligence of the village.

In the initial meetings, Sarvodaya organizers listen as villagers explore what is needed locally. They do not come in with blueprints for change, although they may have private beliefs about what task the village should accomplish. The task, however, is not the main point; the process of village transformation is to move from selfishness, squabbling, and passivity, to competence, confidence, and a heightened spiritual awareness. Organizers at these initial meetings not only listen, but they model listening for other villagers who may not have really heard each other for years. The meetings provide a setting where a broad cross-section of villagers can speak about what their needs are and listen to each other.

Being listened to in this way builds individual and collective self-esteem within the village. Villagers are no longer infantilized and patronized, but are acknowledged for their experience and competence at whatever level this may exist. It is crucial that organizers really believe in the value of each person's experience, however limited. As individual villagers come to shed some of their feelings of inferiority, as the village itself discovers its collective self-esteem, so then does the "under-developed" country as a whole see itself with new eyes, as more and more villages within Sri Lanka are touched by Sarvodaya. Image is very powerful, and the sense many in the Third World have that they are borne along in a world they have not made and cannot affect, that sense of helplessness, inferiority and rage, is countered by the experience of community and competence that the Sarvodaya movement offers.

At this point it should be noted that even *survival* requires innovation, change, and movement out of one's niche. Much planning in the past, however, has been niche-bound and static. At the beginning of our lives, almost anything is possible. Our "growth" narrows and tunnels our development into constricted channels. This focusing and elimination of alternatives is often seen as maturity. Certainly it simplifies the world. But in cutting out and cutting off parts of ourselves, we cripple what remains. We sacrifice vitality and freedom. Movements like Sri Lanka's Sarvodaya reawaken dormant energies and recover neglected and unnourished abilities. This self-help movement also addresses human needs on multiple levels at once. It does not fill what Abraham Maslow identifies as the lower needs—the basics of hunger, shelter, and so forth—before addressing the higher needs. Such a hierarchy is a Western idea, expressed most cogently in Bertolt

Brecht's *"Erst kommt das fressen, denn kommt die Morale."* ("First comes food, then morality.") Sarvodaya, however, addresses human needs on multiple levels at once. It does not focus technically, it does not specialize, and it does not exclude in order to act, as so much Western science does.

The Sarvodaya Movement identifies Ten Basic Needs, but it does not arrange them in a hierarchy. It does not preach that creature needs must be met before higher needs are, but approaches them simultaneously and holistically. Ariyaratne writes that the satisfaction of these needs is essential to human well-being. They include water, food, housing, clothing, health care, communication, fuel, education, a clean, safe, beautiful environment, and a spiritual and cultural life. Sarvodaya also sees itself in global terms: using the Buddhist concept of awakening, it envisions a process of awareness from the personal to the world-wide level. This very description, introducing the movement to the great majority of readers who have never heard of it, can be seen as part of the world-wide awakening the movement fosters.

Ariyaratne promotes change on all levels at once. He writes that fundamental simultaneous change should take place in three areas:

> Firstly in the area of ideas, of values, of ideologies. Secondly in the area of methods and techniques that our people adopt in their day-to-day life, whether in the field of education, in the field of agriculture, in the field of cottage industries or in anything else. Thirdly, a change in the institutions beginning from village level to the national and international level. I say that there should be a simultaneous change, a change at the same time in the three spheres—of ideas, ideologies and values; a change in the methods and techniques; a change in the organizations and institutions. (A.T. Ariyaratne. *Collected Works, I*, p.11.)

Finally, and integral to the entire movement, are its spiritual principles. Here the goals are to awaken from the "poisonous" states of greed, hatred, fear, ignorance and delusion into awareness and compassion. It is perhaps these spiritual goals that most Westerners, with our institutional separation of church and state and our setting of religion into special houses to be visited only on certain holy days, may find it most difficult to comprehend. In what school of public health or Peace Corps training program are these spiritual goals taught as integral to the planning effort? Planning is one thing, spirituality another, and most of us tend to see religious affiliation or preoccupation as an idiosyncratic, slightly embarrassing, and above all *private* hobby to

which certain of our friends are unaccountably prone. Most Westerners look upon spiritual values as part of the public, political life of a
community with suspicion and distaste. Given our history of religious
strife, intolerance, coercion, and terror, such an attitude is understandable. And yet, one can view the agitation for prayers in the schools of
the United States today or even the more extreme actions by the
radical Christian right as incomplete and misguided attempts to bring
spirituality back into our lives and into our political discourse. The
question we in the West face is how to reintegrate spirituality into our
public and private lives without succumbing to the repressive legislation and doctrinal disputes that have left generations of Westerners
with negative attitudes toward spirituality and organized religion.

At a recent meeting of the American Psychiatric Association I
became aware of a division into body, mind, and spirit. In the largest
meeting were those concerned with the body, with medications and
the "drug trade." Those concerned with this version of the mind were
crowded into the discussions of the economics of the field, an alphabet
soup of financial arrangements. Down in the lower depths, three floors
down in the Hotel Bonaventure were small groups of 20 or so talking
about ethics, healing, the needs of patients, and similar spiritual issues.
These core issues that had to do with the essence of humanity were
considered, by contrast with the chemotherapy of the mind, to be "of
little consequence." I do not mean to demean psychiatry by noting
this. Such a shunting aside of ethics and spirituality occurs everywhere
in Western society.

And yet when we look at a movement like the Sarvodaya self-help
movement, we can recognize that an indispensable and very powerful
part of the invisible infra-structure that makes it strong and successful
are the spiritual resources inherent in this ancient culture. We, with
our own more fragmented and disparate religious history in the West,
face a greater challenge to integrate the spiritual dimension into our
political, social, educational, and physical lives, but there are signs
that such an attempt is being made.

One such sign is the emergence of a group known as the Communications Era Task Force, which, over the past twenty years has circu-
lated a number of publications signed by prominent Western intellec-
tuals, including Linus Pauling, H. Stuart Hughes, Dwight Macdonald,
Robert Heilbroner, and Gunnar Myrdal. The most recent of these
documents, *At the Crossroads,* grew out of a meeting in July 1983 of
some 30 people involved in community renewal efforts. *At the Crossroads* was written because "many of those present felt that a new set

of commonly held hopes, values and visions were emerging and the time had come to articulate these ideas." (*At the Crossroads,* p. 2)

The central message of this document derives from the lesson learned from the Chinese language that every crisis represents both danger and an opportunity, and that our culture has, in looking at its future, concentrated on the dangers of our situation and given scant expression to the opportunities. The authors contend that this negative focus is in itself a danger and may move historical events in the very directions dreaded. The goal of this document, then, is to present new images of reality and more positive visions of the future, so that action may be in positive directions. "As we see our future, so we act. . . . We can bring about desirable changes when we see new directions and act to achieve them." (*At the Crossroads,* p. 5)

Thus for example, the crises of our times, unemployment, growing educational and medical costs, ecological stress, and nuclear terror can be seen as chances for fundamentally rethinking and restructuring our perceptions of work, health, the use of the environment, and the ways to resolve international conflicts so that there may be peace. The book is a collective attempt at positive visualization.

The values stressed by the American Communications Era Task Force, although not explicitly spiritual, bear striking resemblance to many of those preached and practiced by the Sri Lanka Sarvodaya Movement. The first of these values stresses interconnection and cooperation as a new human polity to replace the competitive, individualistic ethos of the modern West. Here the authors draw on contemporary science, especially physics, to point out that the isolation and distinctness of objects is an illusion and, extending this to the human sphere, that the separateness and isolation of the individual—on which competitive industrial capitalism was based—is also illusory. This recognition is remarkably close to the Buddhist teaching of "co-dependent origination" on which so much of the Sarvodaya ethic is based. The authors add that there are other developments in modern technology that "shrink" or interconnect the world, especially in electronic communication. They conclude:

> We are finding that attempts to "conquer" and "exploit" nature make us victims of our own actions rather than victors. . . . We will realize that it does not make sense to make ourselves, our families, our communities or our nation secure by acting in ways that make others less secure. Instead, we can focus on actions which make others more secure, thereby increasing our own security and enhancing our freedom. (p. 13)

Secondly, *At the Crossroads* preaches balance, personal commitment, lifelong learning, and the transcending of professional specialization so that experts are no longer in charge.

Instead, their role is to give others the information and tools to empower them to make their own decisions. As in the Sarvodaya Movement, self-reliance on the part of clients or employees, whether these be Sri Lankan villagers or civil servants or inner city welfare beneficiaries, is a core principle. To empower clients is to release enormous quantities of human energy not available when people are constrained to act as passive recipients of expertise and supervision.

Other shifts involve a change in emphasis from medicine to health as a central focus, (a subject that receives extensive treatment elsewhere in this book) from courts to mediation, from police patrols to block watches, and from commercial banking to lender-directed banking. Perhaps the most important change they recommend, in terms of the central themes of the present study, has to do with their final point. *At the Crossroads* says that we must move from hierarchy to participative management, because changes in the nature of both production and management have made such a shift necessary and desirable.

Can participative management work? Apparently. A striking entrepreneurial venture that embodied many of these values, including participative management, empowered employees, and client choices, was the dramatically successful new airline, People Express. Its founder and president, Donald Burr, wrote, "Most organizations frustrate people who really want to work. They control them, watch them and check up on them. They consider them guilty until proven innocent." (Tarrytown Letter, August 1984, p. 13) Burr treated People's employees differently, and, for the first years, achieved a very high 80% load factor on People's flights by offering a low cost service with choices about the expensive frills most airlines routinely provide.

How was this achieved? The central principle was to be open and generous with employees and passengers and to trust them to work in the absence of expensive layers of management supervision. Every employee was required to own at least 100 shares of the company on the principle that people would work harder for something in which they have a stake than if they are simply working for a paycheck. Many employees became rich from this stockholding requirement.

Secondly, routinization and boredom were avoided by the principle of cross utilization, that is, job rotation. Even top management could collect fares in-flight, and other jobs rotated freely. This kept people fresh, and it helped to foster the attitude of participation and mutual responsibility that was the hallmark of this airline. There was no incentive to shirk work with the excuse that "it's not in my job description."

Finally, there were no supervisors at People Express. As in the Puritan villages of New England, all in the community were responsible for the "salvation" of all. Managers managed themselves, although they did belong to teams that served as a communication network between Burr and the employees so that ideas flowed freely throughout the company.

People Express attempted to revolutionize its internal, employer-employee structure, but it initially proved that participatory management works. The airline was remarkably successful. Trust worked there. The managers at People Express voluntarily shared power, and everyone benefited.

In a recent study of America's best-run corporations, Thomas J. Peters and Robert H. Waterman show that the principles that have made People Express successful have also helped such giants as IBM and Hewlett-Packard. It should be noted that few companies carried these principles as far as People Express did. The key to success, Peters and Waterman write, is to treat employees as adult partners, to trust them, and to give them room to control their own work and to innovate. They write,

> There was hardly a more pervasive theme in the excellent companies than *respect for the individual*. That basic belief and assumption were omnipresent. But like so much else we have talked about, it's not any one thing—one assumption, belief, statement, goal, value, system, or program—that makes the theme come to life. What makes it live at these companies is a plethora of structural devices, systems, styles, and values, all reinforcing one another so that the companies are truly unusual in their ability to achieve extraordinary results through ordinary people. . . . These companies give people control over their destinies. . . .

The completeness and genuineness of this people orientation is expressed in such slogans as Hewlett Packard's "Management by Wandering Around," in other corporate "Jubilees" that celebrate successes and that have ritual components not unlike Sarvodaya's *shramadanas,* in story-telling and myth-making as a form of communication, and in structured peer reviews that foster communal rather than hierarchical evaluation. The authors write, "Nothing is more enticing than the feeling of being needed, which is the magic that produces high expectations. What's more, if it's your peers that have those high expectations of you, then there's all the more incentive to perform well." (*In Search of Excellence,* p. 240)

I will quote more of Peters' and Waterman's lessons about successful management in the face of ambiguity and paradox in my chapter on map-making. I need only note here that, somewhat unusually for business writers, they see expressed and shared values as central to the success of any organization. "Every excellent company we studied is clear on what it stands for, and takes the process of value-shaping seriously. In fact, we wonder whether it is possible to be an excellent company without clarity on values and without having the right sorts of values," they write (p. 280). They quote Philip Selznick who has written, "Leadership fails when it concentrates on sheer survival. Institutional survival, properly understood, is a matter of maintaining values and distinctive identity." (pp. 281–82)

We wonder if some readers might recoil when we talk about trust in corporate management or the hope expressed in the *At the Crossroads* publication or love and compassion in the Sarvodaya movement. Such readers should examine hidden assumptions that foster such squeamishness about positive human energies. In a brilliant article in a recent *Harper's,* Frederick Turner asked his readers if they winced when he wrote of honor, beauty, idealism, and duty. Such squeamishness in Western thought arose, he thought, because:

In the nineteenth century, materialist ethics came together with materialist biology and agreed that there were only two types of rewards: those obviously associated with survival and those obviously associated with reproduction. Two brilliant value systems—Marx's, which reduced all value to the economics of survival, and Freud's, which reduced all value to libido—were the result. . . .

Under the pressure of these theories, which postulated very coarse rewards even for very refined behavior, our value systems changed and coarsened. When people wince at the words "duty," "honor," and "beauty," they are doing exactly what Victorians would have done upon hearing the words "passion," "desire," and "sexuality," or even "money," "fees," and "honoraria." The Victorians, in a last-ditch defense of the older, more complex value system, would naturally have been pained by references to the enemy's rewards. We, the inheritors of D.H. Lawrence and Jean-Paul Sartre, feel the same old blush come to our faces when we are reminded of all the rewards—the joy of duty, the satisfaction of honorable conduct—that we have given up. Not that we are not, often, honorable and dutiful. But we are so in a spirit of taking nasty medicine with good grace, and we are deeply suspicious of those who enjoy doing their duty.

But new discoveries are forcing on us a new value system. The pleasures of eating and sex are not the only rewards. Scientists studying the chemistry of the brain have begun to uncover a remarkable variety of rewards, suppressors of rewards, suppressors of the suppressors, and so on. The pleasures of achievement, of insight into the truth, of heroic exertion or sacrifice, of good conscience, of beauty, are *real* pleasures in themselves, not repressed or sublimated derivatives of libido.

. . . We are starved for the pleasures of the mind and spirit and soul. The twentieth century is full of *angst,* which has its source in a thirst for things like glory, sanctity, conscience, and heroism, things which have been forbidden to us.

Paradoxically, then, materialism as the supreme religion began to sicken when we began to make thinking machines, and died when we began to see ourselves as machines for the production of spirit, soul, value. Materialist politics is dying too, and we have come to see our traditional cultures as machines that support the process of soul-making. All over the world, revolutionary forces are championing complex and traditional value systems—ethnic, religious, and political—against materialism, whether it be liberal, fascist, capitalist, socialist, or communist. What makes the Vietnamese, the Poles, the Afghans, the Palestinians, and the Irish such dangerous adversaries is not a materialist ideology but religion, traditional education, blood ties, patriotism, a sense of beauty, honor, heroism, duty, and all the rest: the endorphins blazing in the head like a lantern, more fiercely than any sexual passion, or thirst, or hunger for bread.

Turner's critique of materialism is limited by its references to the chemistry of the brain to explain the blazing endorphins of nonmaterialist ideology. His attack on the simplistic coarseness of materialist ethics—whether Freud's or Marx's—is nevertheless very telling.

The nascent ethical systems are complex and systemic. Central to the message of the Sarvodaya movement, the Communications Era Task Force and to some extent even creative business ventures such as People Express, is the understanding, symbolized by the satellite pictures of our blue and green planet, that there are no isolated acts. Just as there is no place to stand and observe that does not itself move as time unfolds, so there is also no protected place to act. All that we do and all that we fail to do affects everything. This understanding of interconnection is relatively new to the modern West, many of whose social, political, and even medical theories are still based on a somewhat mechanistic, Newtonian world view in which subject and object are radically separate and "objectivity" is possible. But as a number of recent critiques of the underlying premises of established Western thought have shown, such objectivity, in economics or sociology, for example, actually embodies implicit and undeclared value systems.

Fortunately, the ecology movement, which stresses the delicate web of interconnection, has also shaped our post-Newtonian understanding, as has the development of systems thinking in a number of fields, from psychotherapy to computer science. The fashion for Eastern religions has contributed to this emergent shift in attitude, although the transition from what has been called "linear" thinking to systems thinking is extremely difficult. It is hard for us to learn in our academic specialties that when we divide in order to know, then what we know will be divided. We are baffled when we try to curve the tidy sequences of the line into the contextual richness of the circle. Even our "interdisciplinary" labors at reconnection resemble the futile efforts of the king's horses and king's men who tried to glue the shattered fragments of Humpty Dumpty back together again.

Because our interconnectedness means that there are no isolated acts or even thoughts, then every act done and not done is value-laden. The Communications Era Task Force expresses this insight as follows, "We are interdependent and connected. We now know that every action we take will affect both our environment and our attitudes toward the world, in complex and unpredictable ways." (*At the Crossroads*, p. 11) And Fritjof Capra has made the idea of interconnection central to his description of the emergent values of the "turning point" which he describes in his book of that name.

After a lengthy description and criticism of the implicit values in the "value-free" Western sciences of economics and medicine, Capra writes:

The new vision of reality we have been talking about is based on awareness of the essential interrelatedness and interdependence of all phenomena—physical, biological, psychological, social, and cultural. It transcends current disciplinary and conceptual boundaries and will be pursued within new institutions. . . . The systems view looks at the world in terms of relationships and integration. Systems are integrated wholes whose properties cannot be reduced to those of smaller units. Instead of concentrating on basic building blocks or basic substances, the systems approach emphasizes basic principles of organization. (265–66)

As Capra explains, to understand the complexity of systems will stimulate new behaviors. We are not, as classical Newtonian physics, classical economics, and nineteenth-century biology all proclaimed, isolated integers competing against each other in order to live. Capra writes:

> In classical science nature was seen as a mechanical system composed of basic building blocks. In accordance with this view, Darwin proposed a theory of evolution in which the unit of survival was the species, the subspecies, or some other building block of the biological world. But a century later it has become quite clear that the unit of survival is not any of these entities. *What survives is the organism-in-its-environment.* An organism that thinks only in terms of its own survival will invariably destroy its environment and, as we are learning from bitter experience, will thus destroy itself. From the systems point of view the unit of survival is not an entity at all, but rather a pattern of organization adopted by an organism in its interactions with its environment. (pp. 288–289, emphasis added.)

Advocacy must be replaced by an old Sufi principle, the idea of "reciprocal maintenance." We expect the earth, the sea, the air, plants, animals and other people to maintain us. We have yet to learn that for them to maintain us, we have to maintain in return. It is significant that "primitive" people whose myths visualize their environment as enspirited and alive, disturb it little and maintain their surroundings better than we in the West do. Thus the pygmies whom Colin Turnbull studied, peoples who had lived in the African forest harmoniously for thousands of years, sing to the forest to keep it happy so that it will care for them. They are in a living contact with a living being. They participate in an *I-Thou* dyad, rather than the Western *I-It* by which we relate to nature and often to each other (See Turnbull, *The Forest People;* Berman, *The Re-enchantment of the World;* Carolyn Merchant, *The Death of Nature,* Martin Buber, *I and Thou*).

Seen in the light of this kind of understanding, the Biblical injunction to love one's neighbor as oneself reads not as a pious wish that people be kind but as a powerful and accurate statement about what humanity needs to do in order to survive. Not long ago we heard a Tibetan Buddhist teacher tell some of his students, "It would be all right for people to be selfish if they were only better at it." California youngsters say, "What goes around comes around." Enlightened selfishness means to understand clearly the consequences of one's acts in the complex web of relationships that makes up life in this universe and to act accordingly.

The unit of survival is the organism-in-its-environment, and the individual has no absolute existence apart from this environment. Such awareness of "co-dependent origination" challenges generations of Western individualism and its expression in science, art, education and ethics. It challenges the rancher in Texas who defended his killing of a protected bald eagle because the bird was on his private property. It challenges all legal and philosophical systems that would divide the human world into separate selves and the earth into separately owned bits of property. Native Americans believe that one could no more own the earth than one could own the sky or sea. Buddhists would describe even the attempt so to divide and fragment ourselves and the world as a misguided illusion, the ignorance from which all suffering arises.

One of the strongest statements of this teaching of interconnection has come from Tarthang Tulku, Rinpoche, a Tibetan lama who has worked for over a decade to present Buddhist teachings in a form accessible to Westerners. Tarthang Tulku describes Buddhism not as a religion among many but as an "essentially accurate" description of reality. Tarthang Tulku writes:

> One point is all points. We are in a position in history to see an outward expression of this idea—namely, that we all exist within one world, one planet. We are finally able to know for a certainty that there is no independent or isolated place, unaffected by what happens elsewhere. If resources are depleted or disease appears in one spot, repercussions will be felt elsewhere and on a larger scale. . . . Given such an insight, we have a truly firm basis for motivating altruism and for grounding the idea of 'equality,' a grounding that has not been fully achieved in the past. . . . But if we *see* that each point, each place, each person is truly all others, we will be able to act from a much more enlightened basis. . . . The principle that one point is all points clearly renders impossible all 'self-seeking' that would be to the detriment of others. We no longer discriminate between 'our business' and 'their business.' There is no way for us to ignore what is happening elsewhere as being 'not our business,' or to plead a benign but powerless concern. (*Time, Space and Knowledge,* pp. 301–302)

The "values" that underlie this study, then, are not wishes nor pious hopes, but the attitudes and actions that we must assume as we move beyond individualism and the illusion of separateness to the accurate understanding that if we destroy our environment we destroy ourselves. Compassion, seen in the light of this understanding, is not an effort to be nice to others, not the piety or pity of a sugary faith, but the clear and unavoidable attitude adopted when the nature of reality is understood. What hurts others hurts us. What helps others helps us. There is no separation and no refuge from this interdependence.

Charter

The first International Conference on Health Promotion, meeting in Ottawa this 21st day of November 1986, hereby presents this CHARTER for action to achieve Health for All by the year 2000 and beyond.

This conference was primarily a response to growing expectations for a new public health movement around the world. Discussions focused on the needs in industrialized countries, but took into account similar concerns in all other regions. It built on the progress made through the Declaration on Primary Health Care at Alma Ata, the World Health Organization's Targets for Health for All document, and the recent debate at the World Health Assembly on intersectoral action for health.

Health Promotion

Health promotion is the process of enabling people to increase control over, and to improve, their health. To reach a state of complete physical, mental, and social well-being, an individual or group must be able to identify and realize aspirations, to satisfy needs, and to change or cope with the environment. Health is, therefore, seen as a resource for everyday life, not the objective of living. Health is a positive concept emphasizing social and personal resources, as well as physical capacities. Therefore, health promotion is not just the responsibility of the health sector, but goes beyond healthy life-styles to well-being.

Prerequisite for Health

The fundamental conditions and resources for health are peace, shelter, education, food, income, a stable eco-system, sustainable resources, social justice and equity. Improvement in health requires a secure foundation in these basic prerequisites.

Advocate

Good health is a major resource for social, economic and personal development and an important dimension of quality of life. Political, economic, social, cultural, environmental, behavioral and biological factors can all favour health or be harmful to it. Health promotion action aims at making these conditions favourable through advocacy for health.

Enable
Health promotion focuses on achieving equity in health. Health promotion action aims at reducing differences in current health status and ensuring equal opportunities and resources to enable all people to achieve their fullest health potential. This includes a secure foundation in a supportive environment, access to information, life skills and opportunities for making healthy choices. People cannot achieve their fullest health potential unless they are able to take control of those things which determine their health. This must apply equally to women and men.

Mediate
The prerequisites and prospects for health cannot be ensured by the health sector alone. More importantly, health promotion demands coordinated action by all concerned: by governments, by health and other social and economic sectors, by non-governmental and voluntary organizations, by local authorities, by industry and by the media. People in all walks of life are involved as individuals, families and communities. Professional and social groups and health personnel have a major responsibility to mediate between differing interests in society for the pursuit of health.

Health promotion strategies and programmes should be adapted to the local needs and possibilities of individual countries and regions to take into account differing social, cultural and economic systems.

Health Promotion Action Means:

Build Healthy Public Policy
Health promotion goes beyond health care. It puts health on the agenda of policy makers in all sectors and at all levels, directing them to be aware of the health consequences of their decisions and to accept their responsibilities for health.

Health promotion policy combines diverse but complementary approaches including legislation, fiscal measures, taxation and organizational change. It is coordinated action that leads to health, income and social policies that foster greater equity. Joint action contributes to ensuring safer and healthier goods and services, healthier public services, and cleaner, more enjoyable environments.

Health promotion policy requires the identification of obstacles to the adoption of healthy public policies in non-health sectors, and ways of removing them. The aim must be to make the healthier choice the easier choice for policy makers as well.

Create Supportive Environments

Our societies are complex and interrelated. Health cannot be separated from other goals. The inextricable links between people and their environment constitute the basis for a socio-ecological approach to health. The overall guiding principle for the world, nations, regions and communities alike, is the need to encourage reciprocal maintenance—to take care of each other, our communities and our natural environments. The conservation of natural resources throughout the world should be emphasized as a global responsibility.

Changing patterns of life, work and leisure have a significant impact on health. Work and leisure should be a source of health for people. The way society organizes work should help create a healthy society. Health promotion generates living and working conditions that are safe, stimulating, satisfying and enjoyable.

Systematic assessment of the health impact of a rapidly changing environment—particularly in areas of technology, work, energy production and urbanization—is essential and must be followed by action to ensure positive benefit to the health of the public. The protection of the natural and built environments and the conservation of natural resources must be addressed in any health promotion strategy.

Strengthen Community Action

Health promotion works through concrete and effective community action in setting priorities, making decisions, planning strategies and implementing them to achieve better health. At the heart of this process is the empowerment of communities, their ownership and control of their own endeavors and destinies.

Community development draws on existing human and material resources in the community to enhance self-help and social support, and to develop flexible systems for strengthening public participation and direction of health matters. This requires full and continuous access to information, learning opportunities for health, as well as funding support.

Develop Personal Skills

Health promotion supports personal and social development through providing information, education for health and enhancing life skills. By so doing, it increases the options available to people to exercise more control over their own health and over their environments, and to make choices conducive to health.

Enabling people to learn throughout life, to prepare themselves for all of its stages and to cope with chronic illness and injuries is essential. This has to be facilitated in school, home, work and community settings. Action is required through educational, professional, commercial and voluntary bodies, and within the institutions themselves.

Reorient Health Services

The responsibility for health promotion in health services is shared among individuals, community groups, health professionals, health service institutions and governments. They must work together towards a health care system which contributes to the pursuit of health.

The role of the health sector must move increasingly in a health promotion direction, beyond its responsibility for providing clinical and curative services. Health services need to embrace an expanded mandate which is sensitive and respects cultural needs. This mandate should support the needs of individuals and communities for a healthier life, and open channels between the health sector and broader social, political, economic and physical environmental components.

Reorienting health services also requires stronger attention to health research as well as changes in professional education and training. This must lead to a change of attitude and organization of health services, which refocuses on the total needs of the individual as a whole person.

Moving into the Future

Health is created and lived by people within the settings of their everyday life; where they learn, work, play and love. Health is created by caring for oneself and others, by being able to take decisions and have control over one's life circumstances, and by ensuring that the society one lives in creates conditions that allow the attainment of health by all its members.

Caring, holism and ecology are essential issues in developing strategies for health promotion. Therefore, those involved should take as a guiding principle that, in each phase of planning, implementation and evaluation of health promotion activities, women and men should become equal partners.

Commitment to Health Promotion
The participants in this conference pledge:

• to move into the arena of healthy public policy, and to advocate a clear political commitment to health and equity in all sectors;

- to counteract the pressures toward harmful products, resource depletion, unhealthy living conditions and environments, and bad nutrition; and to focus attention on public health issues such as pollution, occupational hazards, housing and settlements;
- to respond to the health gap within and between societies, and to tackle the inequities in health produced by the rules and practices of these societies;
- to acknowledge people as the main health resource; to support and enable them to keep themselves, their families and friends healthy through financial and other means, and to accept the community as the essential voice in matters of its health, living conditions and well-being;
- to reorient health services and their resources towards the promotion of health; and to share power with other sectors, other disciplines and most importantly with people themselves;
- to recognize health and its maintenance as a major social investment and challenge; and to address the overall ecological issue of our ways of living.

The conference urges all concerned to join them in their commitment to a strong public health alliance.

Call for International Action
The Conference calls on the World Health Organization and other international organizations to advocate the promotion of health in all appropriate forums and to support countries in setting up strategies and programmes for health promotion.

The Conference is firmly convinced that if people in all walks of life, nongovernmental and voluntary organizations, governments, the World Health Organization and all other bodies concerned join forces in introducing strategies for health promotion, in line with the moral and social values that form the basis of this CHARTER, Health For All by the year 2000 will become a reality.

This CHARTER for action was developed and adopted by an international conference, jointly organized by the World Health Organization, Health and Welfare Canada and the Canadian Public Health Association. Two hundred and twelve participants from 38 countries met from November 17 to 21, 1986, in Ottawa, Canada to exchange experiences and share knowledge of health promotion.

The Conference stimulated an open dialogue among lay, health and other professional workers, among representatives of governmental, voluntary and community organizations, and among politicians, administrators, academics and practitioners. Participants coordinated their efforts and came to a clearer definition of the major challenges ahead. They strengthened their individual and collective commitment to the common goal of Health for All by the Year 2000.

This CHARTER for action reflects the spirit of earlier public charters through which the needs of people were recognized and acted upon. The CHARTER presents fundamental strategies and approaches for health promotion which the participants considered vital for major progress. The Conference report develops the issues raised, gives concrete examples and practical suggestions regarding how real advances can be achieved, and outlines the action required of countries and relevant groups.

The move toward a new public health is now evident worldwide. This was reaffirmed not only by the experiences but by the pledges of Conference participants who were invited as individuals on the basis of their expertise. The following countries were represented: Antigua, Australia, Austria, Belgium, Bulgaria, Canada, Czechoslovakia, Denmark, Eire, England, Finland, France, German Democratic Republic, Federal Republic of Germany, Ghana, Hungary, Iceland, Israel, Italy, Japan, Malta, Netherlands, New Zealand, Northern Ireland, Norway, Poland, Portugal, Romania, St. Kitts-Nevis, Scotland, Spain, Sudan, Sweden, Switzerland, Union of Soviet Socialist Republics, United States of America, Wales and Yugoslavia.

* * * * * *

> Now I a fourfold vision see,
> And a fourfold vision is given to me:
> Tis fourfold in my supreme delight
> And threefold in soft Beulah's night
> And twofold Always. May God us keep
> From Single vision and Newton's sleep!

> William Blake

The devil was walking with a friend, who suddenly noted a man picking up something from the ground. With dismay he turned to the Devil and cried, "That man is picking up the truth!" Undismayed, the Devil replied, "Do not fear. All he will do is organize and systematize it!"

Exchange
"How old are you, Mulla?"
"Forty."

"But you said the same the last time I asked you, ten years ago!"
"Yes, I always stand by what I said."

When approached by Werner Erhard for help in understanding problems of food, population, and related matters, Tarzie Vittachi was asked what he had learned in his many years with Subud. (Subud is a world-wide religious group that focuses on practice in which participants, "touched by and open to God," can pursue their own developmental paths.)

Vittachi replied to the head of EST, "Organization kills."

"Why, then," asked Erhard, "were you made head of the organization?"

"To kill any organization that gets created," Vittachi answered.

The Evil Eye

My wife and I went to Morocco when she was expecting a child. She went into a shop and looked at kaftans and very much liked one of them. The price was far too high, and so we left the shop, only to be pursued down the street by the proprietor, who was now trying to give it us for nothing.

I asked him why he should give it away like that.

"Don't you understand?" he shouted. "What kind of people are you? A woman in that condition, when she covets something, puts the evil eye on anyone who doesn't give it to her! I don't want the evil eye!"

I said, "That is absolute nonsense, and you know it!"

"I know it is—but what can I do? You see, I believe it!"

He knew, and he knew that he knew, but he was helpless.

III.

Making the Map

We have no direct access to reality. We have only our maps. Although this book is intended as a practical handbook to bring about healthy social change, the precondition for all such action is mental—a profound shift in perception. The problem with most planning, whether for a household budget or a nationwide health program, is that most of us tend to confuse our maps with reality. We become attached to the static picture we have constructed of things and so cannot see the new possibilities always present in time's rich unfolding. As a consequence, we waste enormous quantities of energy simply defending our maps instead of dealing flexibly with life. We cannot allow changes to challenge our perceptual systems, for our maps offer safety and the illusion that the world is known and navigable and will hold still.

This is not to say that we can do without our maps. Maps are all we have. Apparently, we have no direct access to things as they are. Reality is always a mystery. We must, therefore, have our maps in order to act, but we must always understand that these maps are not reality; they are mere constructions on it, provisional best guesses that are tentative and changeable. We must understand that these maps are instruments, not identities. As Ilya Prigogine has written about the modern physical sciences:

> All description thus implies a choice of the measurement device, a choice of the question asked. In this sense, the answer, the result of the measurement, does not give us access to a given reality. We have to decide which measurement we are going to perform and which question

our experiments will ask the system. Thus, there is an irreducible multiplicity of representations for a system, each connected with a determined
set of operators.

This implies a departure from the classical notion of objectivity, since
in the classical view the only "objective" description is the complete
description of the *system as it is,* independent of the choice of how it is
observed.

We have emphasized the importance of operators because they dem-
onstrate that the *reality studied by physics is also a mental construct;* it
is not merely given. . . . One of the reasons for the opposition between
the "two cultures" may have been the belief that literature corresponds
to a conceptualization of reality, to "fiction," while science seems to
express objective "reality." Quantum mechanics teaches us that the
situation is not so simple. *On all levels reality implies an essential element
of conceptualization.* (Emphasis added) (p. 225–226)

In other words, the soft sciences need not apologize to the hard
sciences for their subjectivity. The conceiving mind intrudes everywhere.

It is when we become ideological about our maps, when we locate
all being and meaning there, and when we stand on them as positions
to defend, that our troubles begin. Then we become desperate, competitive, and inept. Often in such cases we are not even aware of the
hidden assumptions that compel us to speak and act in certain ways;
we know only that we feel unhinged and disoriented when we confront
the unexpected, or angry and impatient at the mistaken views we
perceive at the opposite location. We become *located* against the
enemy, and we can then blame their stupidity, selfishness, and wrong-
headedness when our programs do not work out.

This point might be best illustrated by a story. I still remember a
lecture I delivered some years ago about the Mahayana Buddhist
conception of healing, and a young man who challenged me near the
end of the evening. "Well," he asked, "*Did* the Tibetans have a
tradition of social welfare? Did they take care of these problems?
How?" Behind his intense question lay generations of Western ideas
about what social welfare is and how to go about providing it, and at
the foundation of these ideas lay assumptions about the nature of
matter and meaning. He had an entire, limited and specific map of the
universe, although he may have been unaware of its content and of its
long Western history.

It would be possible, indeed, to trace his preoccupations back to
Plato or the Old Testament. At the shortest range, they harked back to

the reforming tradition of the European and American Scientific Revolution and Enlightenment and the professional history of the institutionalized social sciences, public planning, and public services that emerged and crystallized in the nineteenth and twentieth centuries. These disciplines have seen and manipulated human life in ways that many observers from within and outside our culture have derided as limited, materialistic, and mechanical. Critics also experience the vision of human felicity inherent in these disciplines as truncated. For reasons that go back centuries into the history of religious strife and of scientific and technological development in Europe, the enormous energy of human compassion has been largely channeled in the West into contemporary social and clinical sciences that have been built on a materialist base and set in a desacralized, inert universe that is available for almost unlimited manipulation. In addition, these disciplines and professions have developed in tandem with the modern bureaucratic state, so that their purposes have always been dual: individual welfare mixed inextricably with social control. Our usual definitions of health and our images of what is humanly possible exist for the most part within these impoverishing limits.

As our young questioner made clear in the subsequent discussion, to him social welfare programs meant indoor plumbing, hygiene, a minimum count of protein grams per day, and other humane interventions designed to prevent illness rather than to produce wellness. With Bertolt Brecht, Abraham Maslow, and the dominant culture of the modern West, he carried within his mind an implicit hierarchy of needs in which meaning, beauty, and deity cannot be broached before the lower-order, creature needs have been met. Most striking about his assumptions was the separation of the two orders of needs and the lack of recognition of the interplay and mutual nurturance between them.

We wanted to say to his question that what we perceive as needs are often merely wants. Needs are the basic essentials of life as determined by nature and culture. Wants are creations of dominant ideology and organization. Values, which relate to these issues of need and want, can be both universal and culturally diverse. Multiple constructions on reality exist, so that planners must be careful not to impose—even in their conceptual thinking or mapping—their own culturally or ideologically determined hierarchies of needs and wants. It is essential to remain open to the many alternative visions that inhere in every concern or human endeavor. We might even quote Ilya Prigogine again on the wealth of reality. Prigogine writes:

. . . No single theoretical language articulating the variables to which a well-defined value can be attributed can exhaust the physical content of a system. Various languages and points of view about the system may be complementary. They all deal with the same reality, but it is impossible to reduce them to one single description. The irreducible plurality of perspectives on the same reality expresses the impossibility of a divine point of view from which the whole of reality is visible. . . .

The real lesson to be learned from the principle of complementarity, a lesson that can perhaps be transferred to other fields of knowledge, consists in emphasizing the wealth of reality, which overflows any single language, any single logical structure. Each language can express only part of reality. . . .

As I looked at our young challenger and tried to frame an answer, I had a picture of him blundering with the best possible will into a delicate, balanced, integrated civilization (if any, indeed, remain), trying to offer "social welfare" and inadvertently doing enormous damage. All this would happen because he takes his map to be reality and does not stand outside it. Each belief system expresses only part of reality.

Perhaps this anecdote illustrates the magnitude of this first task, the task that is the essential precondition to all the practical advice that follows. As the history of most academic and professional disciplines makes abundantly clear, even a relatively minor restructuring of a perceptual framework can be very difficult to accomplish. It can be expected to evoke widespread resistance, criticism, and even mockery. *All change evokes resistance: if people are not raising hell about what you are doing, then there is a good chance that you are not doing very much.*

We start, therefore, with the most difficult work. Changing the map can be terrifying. Our belief systems about the organization of things ground us in time and space. They also provide us with security, and not just on the conceptual level. Careers are built on belief systems. We are, therefore, challenging investments when we change maps. People have located themselves according to the established maps; they have built their careers and their houses there. Of course they resist change.

The resistance to change is also built into our very perceptual frame. Anthropologists who have worked on the comparative social construction of reality are familiar with the conservative bias built into the process of perception itself and the culture-wide illusions that what one has learned to see is reality itself. Elizabeth Bowen, in *Return to*

Laughter, describes the amazed response of the New Guinea villagers among whom she worked because she was unable to *see,* let alone name, the more than forty distinct shades of green that were part of their world of perception. Victor Turner summarizes such experiences. "As a member of society, most of us see only what we expect to see, and what we expect to see is what we are conditioned to see when we have learned the definitions and classifications of our culture" (*Forest of Symbols,* p.95). Bowen's villagers, unaware of the cultural component in their seeing, treated their visitor gently and sympathetically, as one who was crippled by a visual handicap.

The following long passages by the British anthropologist, Mary Douglas, deal cogently both with the cultural conservatism built into learned perceptual patterns and with the human resistance to change fostered by our love of "hard lines and clear concepts."

> For it seems that whatever we perceive is organized into patterns for which we, the perceivers, are largely responsible. Perceiving is not a matter of passively allowing an organ—say of sight or hearing—to receive a ready-made impression from without, like a palette receiving a spot of paint. Recognizing and remembering are not matters of stirring up old images of past impressions. It is generally agreed that all our impressions are schematically determined from the start. As perceivers we select from all the stimuli falling on our senses only those which interest us, and our interests are governed by a pattern-making tendency, sometimes called *schema* (see Bartlett, 1932). . . . As learning proceeds objects are named. Their names then affect the way they are perceived next time: once labelled they are more speedily slotted into the pigeon-holes in future.
>
> As time goes on and experiences pile up, we make a greater and greater investment in our system of labels. So a conservative bias is built in. It gives us confidence.

In her conclusion, Douglas muses,

> It is part of our condition that the purity for which we strive and sacrifice so much turns out to be hard and dead as a stone when we get it. . . . Purity is the enemy of change, of ambiguity and compromise. Most of us indeed would feel safer if our experience could be hard-set and fixed in form. As Sartre wrote so bitterly of the anti-Semite:
>
>> "How can anyone choose to reason falsely? It is simply the old yearning for impermeability . . . there are people who are attracted by the permanence of stone. They would like to be solid and impenetrable, they do not want change: for who knows what change might bring? . . ."

This diatribe implies division between ours and the rigid black and white thinking of the anti-Semite. Whereas, of course, the yearning for rigidity is in us all. It is part of our human condition to long for hard lines and clear concepts. (Douglas, p.191)

This love of "hard lines and clear concepts" has distorted not only the perceptions of primitives in New Guinea but the development of many modern Western objective "hard," social, and clinical sciences. One simply cannot *see* or organize material that does not have a place in the learned perceptual map.

In psychotherapy, for example there have been many developments in the last generation that illustrate not only the limiting and stagnant constraints of a single conceptual framework but also the resistance to new models as they emerge. For generations after Freud, his followers treated their clients according to a map that was essentially contained within the patient's mind. The struggle for health was seen as internal, and the job of the therapist was to enable the patient to resolve intra-psychic conflict. This psychoanalytic model is still entrenched orthodoxy in many major training centers even today, especially in medical schools. Evidence that does not fit the model simply cannot be incorporated into the analytic framework and worked on.

When, in the 1950s and 1960s, a number of gifted and independent spirits began to look at the fact that the intra-psychic model was not working in the treatment of severe disorders such as schizophrenia, they began to work to construct other maps, inter-personal maps rather than intra-psychic ones. A number of new schools, including the field of family therapy, emerged at this time. The new systemic framework enabled therapists to inquire what, in the current family system within which clients lived, produced and sustained their symptoms. This interpersonal, current, and non-historical mapping allowed unexpected evidence to emerge into the clinical framework, evidence that had been available but invisible according to the therapist's old intra-psychic map. Now it was possible to see it, organize it systematically, and work with it clinically.

The family therapy or intervention of reframing is a form of remapping that helps clients to crack open their hard lines and clear concepts. It allows them to change by offering them fresh interpretations of old patterns. Neuro-linguistic programmers use similar techniques. A friend of ours who attended a recent NLP seminar reported that when she told the leader she was suffering from depression, he crowed, "That's wonderful! Hey everybody, did you hear that? This lady is depressed. Do you know how much energy she has available when she decides to use it?'' This "pattern interrupt" initially startled and irritated our friend—people had always taken her depressions *seriously*—and then stimulated anger, clarity, activity and relief from her depression. The leader relabeled her behavior, and stimulated a shifting of behavior and attitude that disturbed a depressive cycle of many years standing. A space where change could take place opened between structures. *The changer redefines the structure, draws a new map, and the participants take care of shifting their behaviors on the new gameboard.*

Many of us who supported Cesar Chavez's attempts to organize the California farmworkers in the 1960s and 1970s regarded Safeway as the arch-oppressor, because Safeway bought produce from strike breaking farmers. (We were also boycotting grapes, and an entire generation of Berkeley liberal children grew up without ever tasting a grape.) Safeway as the capitalist oppressor was defined as the bully on the block. But now in the 1980s if Safeway can be seen as a vast resource, an impressively efficient distribution system that can be used to help the poor, new possibilities for action can unfold. Safeway defined as the bad kid in the family will not want to cooperate, but a positive reframe of Safeway as a powerful and efficient friend may mobilize this giant corporation to behave differently. Can the Safeway distribution system be used to deliver goods to the poor in parallel structures to the Safeway stores? Why should Safeway want to do this? Safeway officials, approached as a vast resource, can expand and feel confident, for they have been acknowledged in their own terms for doing what they do well. This is the therapeutic "and" intervention. "Yes, you do this well, *and* you could also do this for the hungry," rather than the scolding and directive, "You have been hurting people for a long time, now you had better start making up for it." The old system of negative labeling does not work, not to end family nagging nor to get Safeway to deliver goods to the poor.

There are many possible maps. The choice of one depends not on accuracy, but on the possibilities for action, confidence, and hope. The right map is the one that permits healthy change. Is it useful to continue to label Safeway as an oppressor or can a redefinition move matters? Reality has multiple maps, but in order to promote change, one needs to start with people as they are, whether they be bullying spouses or bullying corporations. It is useful to start with the client's map, as long as one keeps the larger map in mind. One can seek the positive wish in dysfunctional behavior and communicate it to the client. Change entrepreneurs should at the same time shift readily between the immediate problem, the small client map, and multiple layers of mapping to the widest possible vision. The danger here is that change entrepreneurs will forget the larger view and become drawn into the client's map of things, or that they will become attached to their own large maps and mistake them for reality. Maps are constantly revised as action takes place. Flexibility is essential. All fixed structures express yesterday's realities.

Change entrepreneurs, working with a nest of maps, make repeated diagnostic interventions to determine what level of mapping is appropriate for a given change. The process can be very slow, demanding great patience and flexibility, or it can at times of crisis suddenly open into major shifts. Often the changer will not know what intervention, if any, stimulated a desired goal. We always work with only partial knowledge. Change entrepreneurs cannot even rest on their laurels. They have no property rights in change and no obvious ego gratification. Their loyalty is not to a single institution or a single vision of reality, but to the process of change and the hope for a better world.

One might well ask if this abstract commitment is enough to sustain one for a lifetime of meddling in social and political structures. If there is no fundamental commitment to institution or ideology, then what sustains the change entrepreneur? Where is the community and where the identity? Where is the water to fill the reservoirs of patience?

One can view such meddlers as players in a floating crap game, a game that meets briefly on the street to play, always ready to move on to a new location when the law descends. In all institutions, such people exist; they slide between the structures, work outside established channels, and avoid getting mired in institutional loyalties or fixed routines. It is for such people that this book is being written, to encourage them and to let them know that they have a *Sangha,* a diffuse community of slippery characters like themselves. Similar people with common humanistic values, they have the capacity to communicate with each other on multiple levels. They are basically *clinicians,* meddlers for growth and change. Rule-breakers and risk-takers, they are uncomfortable within institutional constraints and fixed disciplines, although they often function within such confines for much of their careers. In fact, they can be distinguished from dilettantes and misfits by their mastery of a particular discipline before they move into their floating modality. One could say that they are sustained by their own quirkiness, but this makes their identities too narcissistic. They are not different for the sake of being different.

Theirs is not an aesthetic exercise, a subtle presentation of self. These meddlers are *genuinely* odd ducks, what folklorists would identify as Tricksters, Coyotes, or Fools.

The following anecdote concerns such a change meddler.

A friend of ours, high in government but not involved with the military, was invited to "war games." He was the President of the U.S.A. The other teams were China, Russia, India, Pakistan and others. The battle was fought out as the Chinese came over Bhutan into India. Instead of the usual response, our friend pulled back fleets, showered the Indians and Chinese with food and radios, and assisted others to talk and work things out. The computers said the U.S. won the war. Pakistan and India became friends. China withdrew. A new detente occurred.

When invited to the debriefing, we watched in amazement as a representative of the Air Force addressed his military, C.I.A., State Department and White House colleagues, and said, "Mr. X, you won but you will never be asked into the war games again. You didn't play by the rules! Even the Chinese generals play by the rules." He never was asked again, for as a "spoilsport" he was treated like a leper. Even the cheat is more acceptable. He jumped, he was closer to the truth, but as the Devil said, "Have no fear, the truth will be organized and systematized. There is no cause for worry."

One way to identify such colleagues for change, apart from the instant, multi-level snap of recognition that can stimulate such people to greet each other as "You're one of us!" is to look at those who have stayed out of institutional clinches and have made lateral career shifts. Such people often go from the core of a demanding discipline into a related field and have moved back and forth into and out of related disciplines, fields, and institutions. Their search for like-minded spirits can be a lonely one, for they are often viewed by the orthodox with suspicion and dislike. Their essence is movement not stasis, and when they find others who move in the same way, they are at home.

This flowing or watery quality makes the metaphor of mapping somewhat misleading, except for those superb maps that portray flow, as in the *Times Atlas of World History* (Hammond, Maplewood, New Jersey, 1984, 2nd edition) which show population movements, the great migrations of people and animals and plants through Earth's history. This is the ideal map, for most maps are frozen and static structures, whereas change entrepreneurs need to be in constant motion, constantly revising images of reality, and enlarging and modifying the realm in which they function.

The Buddhist conception of the vehicle may be a more telling image for what we mean than the idea of a map. The vehicle, although a structure such as a boat, a car, wings, or legs, is designed to move and to carry its passenger. Vehicles may not only move at varying speeds, and they change direction. And different vehicles are appropriate to different situations. Buddhists often play with the idea of a spiritual vehicle as a boat, able to control direction to some extent while crossing the river, and yet also constrained by the current. Those who fight the river defeat themselves and become exhausted, whereas those who merely drift, who "go with the flow", are not fully human, active, and alive. Nor do they reach the opposite bank! The middle way is the skillful one, an elusive balance between self-defeating, excessive, and ignorant action and passive, dull-witted acquiescence.

The vehicle is useful, necessary, and indispensable. One cannot move without it. Skillful action, however, means to choose a vehicle that is appropriate for the path. A boat impedes progress if you are climbing a mountain. And yet, enormous numbers of people drag their boats up dusty paths and wear themselves out lugging them up mountains.

The idea of discarding the vehicle is a commonplace in many religious traditions. One Buddhist scholar describes it as follows:

Thus far, we have been considering methods, not final aims. In both Don Juan's view and Buddhism, a disciple or apprentice who experientially enters into a radically different perceptual world in order to turn back the wheel of life or stop the world has not necessarily attained "insight wisdom" or "seeing"; he is only on the brink of attaining it. This stage in the path of the learner is the most difficult, for he has to take the next step alone; the teachings can do no more than lead him up to the point of breakthrough. That is why the Buddhist stresses the importance of a seeker's *vow* to attain Enlightenment; he must have utter conviction to pursue the Path to the end.

The Buddhist speaks of "killing the Buddha" at this stage in the Path; that is, of discarding the raft of teachings once it has helped the disciple to cross the river of ordinary life. The danger is that he will want to hold on to the raft. But he must not. He must cast it aside, must empty himself not only of the nominalistic, relativized description of the world, but also of the teachings of the emptiness of all things. Buddhist teachings are only techniques, *means* to the attainment of wisdom, not definitions of the Real. The Buddhist does not attempt to define the Real. He denies the possibility of a definition by asserting that Nirvana *is* samsara, that the state of Enlightenment *is* the state of ordinary existence.

[Daniel Noel. *Seeing Castaneda: Reactions to the "Don Juan" Writings of Carlos Castaneda.* Capricorn Books. Putnam G.P. Putnam's Sons NY 1976 James W. Boyd, "The Teachings of Don Juan from a Buddhist Perspective," DISCARDING THE RAFT (226–227)]

There is a crucial question of selection and timing here. Buddhists have a saying that you should not burn your boat until you have crossed the river. The flexibility that planners need must be accompanied by steadiness, balance, and wisdom. They need to be able to change quickly, but they also need to know when not to change, when to stay in the boat. Until that golden day when we all reach enlightenment, we cannot afford to burn our boats until other vehicles are available.

An example of tragic vehicle burning occurred during the reforms in American mental health in the 1960s and 1970s, as thousands and thousands of severely afflicted individuals were released from asylums and other institutions with the hope that they could be brought into a community mental health setting, an outpatient network that would give them support and nurturance without confining them unnecessarily. The idea was exciting, but planners burned the old boat before creating a new vehicle, and the result has been that many—too many— people who could be safe are floundering in the river, that is to say, sleeping in shelters, under bridges or in jails, cut loose from institutional support with no place to go. These victims were *deconnected,* fragmented, and inadvertently isolated by this tragedy of timing.

The question of choosing a vehicle in order to act is separate, however, from the prior process of *map making.* Change entrepreneurs think years ahead of action; they need their maps to be ahead of events, even in the great majority of cases where they will not be acting on them. Let us then return to the metaphor of the map, the projective map, the map of the future.

In constructing future maps, change entrepreneurs want to be far enough ahead of events, and to have enough alternative tomorrows in mind so that events do not unduly startle them. They need to insulate themselves from being merely reactive and hitting back when they are hit. All action has unintended consequences, but flexible planners, if they allow a free imagination to range over the future, should have conceived of many of them.

I refer to Buddhist stories to make points about planning in the 1980s. If this seems odd to readers, I ask them to look at the belief systems—the conscious and half-conscious maps of reality—that would exclude such wisdom from their calculations. What I say here is not new, only forgotten, or more accurately, set aside. In bookstores and libraries, folktales are placed aisles away from serious works on public health and planning, preserved as fossils from a human past we have transcended. I offer some such stories here, as they relate to the issues I have discussed—of the need to let go of outdated maps, and of the violence that can be done when the mind distorts reality—to illumine these issues.

The first is a Buddhist tale, from a patriarchal Southeast Asian Buddhist tradition in which monks were forbidden to touch women.

> Two Buddhist monks on their way to the monastery, found a . . . woman at the riverbank. Like them, she wished to cross the river, but the water was too high. So one of the monks lifted her onto his back and carried her across.
>
> His fellow monk was thoroughly scandalized. For two hours he berated him on his negligence in keeping the rule: Had he forgotten he was a monk? How did he dare touch a woman? And worse, carry her across the river? What would people say? Had he not brought their holy religion into disrepute? And so on.
>
> The offending monk patiently listened to the never-ending sermon. Finally he broke in with "Brother, I dropped that woman at the river. Are you still carrying her?"

The second such story concerns Nasruddin, a loveable Sufi anti-hero who consistently gets into scrapes because he is pig-headed, self-righteous, and ignorant. Here he has reached a high position and is, as always, meddling.

> Nasruddin became prime minister to the king. Once, while he wandered through the palace, he saw a royal falcon. Now Nasruddin had never seen this kind of a PIGEON BEFORE. So he got out a pair of scissors and trimmed the claws, the wings, and the beak of the falcon. "Now you look like a decent bird," he said. "Your keeper had evidently been neglecting you."

Another Sufi tale concerns a do-gooding monkey.

> "What on earth are you doing?" said I to the monkey when I saw him lift a fish from the water and place it on a tree.
>
> "I am saving it from drowning" was the reply.

The monkey intervened where he should not, and the upshot was a dead fish in a tree. A modern story about garbage points the opposite moral; here, rigid thinking prevented action where action was possible, and the upshot was rats in the kitchen.

When I worked for the Department of Health and Urban Development (HUD) we were concerned about the problem of rat control in the housing projects. A major program of the Public Health Service was dedicated to their removal. Narrowly focused, this program sought the rat poison that worked best.

The rat problem, however, broadened into a larger map. We asked who picked up the garbage, how often, and from what sites. Investigators quickly blamed the victims, the residents who were plagued by rats, telling them that they had dirty habits. But, of course, even the most fastidious residents suffered from the rats, so clearly more was at stake.

Because of the problems we found with garbage storage and pick-up, we recommended that garbage disposals be put into the apartments. Studies showed that this would cut collection costs, diminish loose food contaminants, and eliminate the risks attendant on spreading rat poisons around where children might get into them.

Resistance within the department to this solution was immediate and vocal. No! These people cannot have disposals. Disposals would be broken. Many employees confided that they did not have disposals at home, so they did not want the poor in the housing projects to get such amenities. The idea was dropped fast.

The resistance to change arose from a deep conviction that the poor are undeserving. As a consequence, the rat infestation continued, and the costs of control mounted. The attempts to expand the map floundered on the prejudices of the clean and respectable employees of this Washington bureaucracy. I read recently that rats had attacked and severely injured a baby in the kitchen of one such housing project apartment.

In the HUD story, the issue was map expansion, and the blockage arose from belief systems. The following account, from the tales of the psychotherapist Milton Erickson, shows how a habitual pattern of behavior was interrupted by a very modest change in scale and direction of a map. As with the previous account, the intervention provoked lively resistance, but here it was overcome.

A woman came to see me and she said, "I weigh 180 pounds. I've dieted successfully under doctors' orders hundreds of times. And I want to weigh 130 pounds. Every time I get to 130 pounds I rush into the kitchen to celebrate my success. I put it back on right away. Now I weigh 180.

Can you use hypnosis to help me reduce to 130 pounds? I'm back to 180 for the hundredth time.

I told her, yes, I could help her reduce by hypnosis, but she wouldn't like what I did.

She said she wanted to weigh 130 pounds and she didn't care what I did.

I told her she'd find it rather painful.

She said, "I'll do anything you say."

I said, "All right. I want an absolute promise from you that you will follow my advice exactly."

She gave me the promise very readily and I put her into a trance. I explained to her again that she wouldn't like my method of reducing her weight and would she promise me, absolutely, that she would follow my advice? She gave me that promise.

Then I told her, "Let both your unconscious mind and your conscious mind listen. Here's the way you go about it. Your present weight is now 180 pounds. I want you to gain twenty pounds and when you weigh 200 pounds on my scale, you may start reducing."

She literally begged me, on her knees, to be released from her promise. And every ounce she gained she became more and more insistent on being allowed to start reducing. She was markedly distressed when she weighed 190 pounds. When she was 190 she begged and implored to be released from her own promise. At 199 she said that was close enough to 200 pounds and I insisted on 200 pounds.

When she reached 200 pounds she was very happy that she could begin to reduce. And when she got to 130 she said, "I'm never going to gain again."

Her pattern had been to reduce and gain. I reversed the pattern and made her gain and reduce. And she was very happy with the final results and maintained that weight. She didn't want to, ever again, go through that horrible agony of gaining twenty pounds.

This last case reveals that when time is short, goals clear, and the scale small, precise planning with predictable outcomes can occur. Erickson's clever paradoxical intervention achieved a clear goal in a relatively short period of time. For this reason, planning entrepreneurs *think globally, act locally*. Their multiple maps cover the largest possible range in both space and time. In constructing future maps, planners need to see far enough ahead of the present to envision enough alternative tomorrows so that events do not unduly startle them. They also need to insulate themselves from being merely reactive, hitting back when events hit them. All action has unintended consequences, but flexible planners will have allowed their imagination to range freely over the future and will have anticipated many of them.

In addition, planning entrepreneurs need to *go to strange places to get information.* In order to scent emergent trends, planners need to avoid standard information systems and bypass some ideas that are in good currency. To plan for change, the usual mechanisms of information gathering do not work, because they depend on "yesterday's news." Standard information systems can also overwhelm planners with the sheer bulk of undigested data. The library in the Psychology Department at the University of California at Berkeley, for example, receives over 2,000 journals in the field of psychology, and the reference librarian notes that even these do not cover the field. We choke on our information. No one can "keep up."

"We do not know more about mankind than ancient philosophers did, although we have more details." (Eugen Weber, p. 13) The details to which historian Weber refers, that vast accumulation of data that we have built up, especially in the last generation or so, can actually serve as an obstacle to planning. The very bulk of material can block action, as anyone who has worked in a large office or bureaucracy can testify. Paper—square, opaque, and amazingly heavy in mass—dams the flow of change. Even the more quick and flexible computer storage discs can foster an illusion of competence and mastery for those who have access to them.

It is said often that this is the information age, that what we buy and sell is information, and that even money is no longer a hard reality grounded in buried bullion, but only another information bit. But what is all this information, what does it tell us about human values, purposes, and planning, and according to what system is this information structured? Although it may not be true to assert that in this modern age we know more and more about less and less, there is absolutely no evidence that gathering more data and fitting it into the old conceptual structures aids us to understand the human present and to envision a human future and a way to reach it.

In making the map, then, the planners do not collect new data. Data is usually collected and arranged according to existent and possibly obsolete models. Because our period is one in which rules are changing, however, it is to these conceptual shifts that planners must direct their attention. The organizing principles are changing so rapidly that no single set is useful to understand a given problem. Therefore, planners must develop the mental agility to view a given problem according to several sets of rules, several models of reality, and through many lenses, from the close-up lens to the wide-angle and zoom.

The following case study illustrates the unorthodox process of information gathering necessary to make maps for change. It also shows that when one is collecting data, one is also intervening. Some years ago, in an attempt to discover what contributed to mental health in a city, a team of us from the U.S. National Institute of Mental Health "scouted" Detroit.

Before the first visit, we telephoned friends in and out of the Detroit government in order to make informal contact with some key Detroit residents. We allowed the purpose of our visit to be floated through the network of contacts, so that important actors such as the mayor heard that we were coming. On arrival we met with the mayor and his staff, who asked each of us, individually and alone, why we were there. I heard years later that our stories agreed not only with each other but were consistent with the informal intelligence the mayor's staff had acquired through the story (true) we had floated and that they were therefore willing to open their doors to us.

We visited Detroit many times. Each time, we mapped out the city and the mental health issues. What was particularly striking in those days was that the interlocking power structures, although differing in views, worked on the same gameboard or map of the city. Each understood their interrelationships in the same way. Regularly, too, many of their leaders met in the Metropolitan Club to discuss emerging issues.

Then, on a later visit, another striking phenomenon became apparent when our team discovered an almost "science-fiction" like situation. The map was no more. Now although each special group occupied the same physical space, they lived in different conceptual worlds. We went to the mayor's chief assistant and asked what was wrong, because it appeared that Detroit would explode or disintegrate. The mayor seemed to be involved in a family difficulty and appeared to be too preoccupied to make the connections between the varied groups. Although the reasons for Detroit's difficulties were very complex and related to urban issues we see today, this inability to connect the players played a role in the explosion that came in the riots just a few months later. A disjointed map is an important sign that trouble is afoot.

In this case, it was not the data that helped us diagnose the problem, but the structure of things, the way the parts fit together. The tenuous connecting link, the mayor, distracted by his personal concerns, no longer functioned.

Often one diagnoses a situation by means of unobtrusive measures that can function as flags to the observer that something big is wrong. First impressions, sensory impressions of the general atmosphere of a place, provide valuable clues. When entering an institution, smell the cafeteria or check for trash in the stairwells. A sour kitchen and littered stairs are indications that the system may be working badly. Such clues are available even at a distance. When cables came from the Peace Corps in the Philippines to Washington that the jeeps were breaking down, we knew that more than the jeeps were working badly. Jeeps can be fixed locally when a human system is working and communication pathways are functioning. The cables told us that the bigger map of human interaction in the Philippines Peace Corps had become disjointed and fragmented. This lack of communication, this inability to play on the same gameboard, had escalated a minor problem, the malfunctioning of the jeeps, to the highest level of tension. Family court judges are called upon to render decisions on similarly minor issues every day, such issues as who should take a child to the ballet on Saturday because the fundamental structure of the institution, the family, no longer functions.

Once Peace Corps headquarters in Washington determined that there was a real problem in the Philippines, they needed further information about what was wrong. Sargent Shriver, then director of the Peace Corps, became convinced he probably would have to fire the director when he heard that the volunteers were living in "splendor" with a swimming pool. Other things had been going wrong as well, including a high dropout rate by volunteers. Shriver's response was direct and immediate. First he would go to the Philippines, which he did, and then he would fire the director.

Trying to find out what was going on, I took my coffee cup and walked on a one-day tour through the Peace Corps building [in Manila], starting on floor 12. As I wandered through the building, chatting informally, it became clear that the staff had a tremendous amount of information. From each I found out a part [of the story]. A full visit to the Philippines was not absolutely necessary. I learned that day that the Philippines project idea had come from the Peace Corps Deputy Director, whose father had failed in a missionary program in the Philippines years before; the contract for training volunteers went to the group that had completed a feasibility study that said it was unfeasible; and the Director was chosen at the last minute because of tremendous pressure from the White House. By completing the 12-story day, I learned that the problem could not be solved by firing the Director nor by visiting the site for a few days.

The newly hired head psychiatrist went to the Philippines with Mr. Shriver and saw that this was true. The solution was to change the project, the staff and the volunteers gradually in order to create a new system. This solution was effective. *Moral:* there are many ways to learn about a problem by piecing it together and unorthodox ways can be useful. Gossip can be a tool. Reframing the picture works better than curing one symptom at a time. Other ways to do "quick and dirty" assessments that will give you a rough general idea of the big map include going to such unorthodox sources for hard information as the women's pages of a newspaper, real estate agents, hospital newsletters, and policemen. The women's pages in many cities will give you the city power structure right in the society columns, and the repeated names in institutional newsletters will often do the same. To learn about a city from real estate agents, go to three different agents in different parts of town looking for a house and inquiring about good and bad neighborhoods, schools, services, ethnic mix, and so on. The agents know it all, but by asking three of them, you get varied views— the Rashomon effect—of the same city. You can do this in less than an hour with each agent, so you are not wasting a great deal of their time. If you can get a patrolman talking about the city, of course, it is all there, and the same is true for public health nurses, sales people, and anyone who moves around in a given setting. Again, remember that you are seeking connections and structure, the map, not hard and precise data. Often the gossip you hear will be inaccurate and you must allow for this, but if you question enough people you can still get a surprisingly accurate picture of the total scene.

I conclude this chapter with two stories.

They asked Helmi

Why do you take so much interest in matters that are not connected with the progress of men?

He said: When you want to know how the coppersmith has been working, you look at the shavings on the floor.

And from the Sufi tales:

There was a countryman who had sold his watch because he told a visitor the trains ran on time within earshot and therefore he did not need one.

"But how do you tell the time, say, in the early hours of the night, when there are no trains?"

"That's easy. I have a bugle by my bed. When I want to know the time at night I blow it hard, as loud as I can, out of the window. Someone always shouts: "Who's that fool making such a noise at ten past three in the morning?"

* * * * * *

Robert Kennedy said:

The gross national product includes air pollution and cigarette advertising and ambulances to clear our highways of carnage. It includes the destruction of the redwoods, and the death of Lake Superior. It includes locks for our doors, and jails for the people who break them. It swells with the production of napalm and nuclear warheads, and armored cars for the police to put down riots in our cities. It counts Whitman's rifle and Speck's knife, and television programs that glorify violence the better to sell toys to our children.

Yet if it counts all this, there is much that it does not include. It does not allow for the health of our children, the quality of their education or the joy of their play. It ignores the beauty of our poetry and the strength of our marriages, the intelligence of our public debate and the integrity of our public officials. It measures neither our wit nor our courage, neither our wisdom nor our learning, neither our compassion nor our devotion to country. It measures everything, in short, except that which makes life worthwhile.

I also owe my thanks to those other colleagues who responded to my ideas with embarrassment, indignation, resentment, open rejection, or anxiety. Without such reactions I would not have realized so clearly that I was treading on taboo territory and would not have hit upon the idea of analyzing the background of these taboos.

Alice Miller
Thou Shalt Not Be Aware

There is the story of the fighting couple who came to the Rabbi, each with their tale of woe. Each separately told the Rabbi what the problem was with the other.

To each he replied, "You're right!"

His wife, overhearing his discussion, asked, "How could you tell them both that they were right?"

Turning to his wife he said, "You're right, my dear!"

IV.

Rules for Change Entrepreneurship: A Handbook

The first stage in social change is internal, the mental shakeup and rethinking described in the map-making chapter above. *The map-making process does not stop once action has begun;* there is a constant interplay between vision and action. Any map that becomes too static hampers action. So does a fixed commitment to a precise desired outcome. Therefore, although thinking and acting are, for purposes of clarity, presented separately here, they do not occur in sequence. It is crucial to keep this point in mind in order to avoid falling into old patterns such as *"Make the plan: implement it,"* for these planning patterns have repeatedly proven ineffective.

Planning entrepreneurs work as irritants in fixed systems. Although they may have certain goals in mind, they remain flexible about details. Their role is to stir the pot. Once the forces for change have been set in motion, entrepreneurs must understand that what happens will be partly out of their control. This is to be expected; it is not to be deplored. Planning entrepreneurs stimulate human energies that create change, and although many of these are creative and positive, other energies—greed, fear, territoriality—can also be activated. Once this is clearly understood, these forces can be used skillfully. *It hampers change to label certain groups or individuals as enemies whose energies need to be suppressed or bypassed.*

Rule number one for planning entrepreneurs, then, is to avoid territoriality. Planning entrepreneurs must abandon ownership of their ideas, for as soon as a plan becomes known as the "Jones Plan," it becomes fixed in content and located personally. Polarization almost inevitably follows. This rule, however, is difficult to follow, for the entrepreneur has just spent a great deal of energy liberating his or her mind from fixed concepts and outdated maps. Having opened one's intelligence to a large map and creative visions of the future, the planner now must implement this vision without getting credit for it! It seems too much to ask. However, if the planner has done his or her conceptual work at all well, it is possible that the ideas that have emerged or descended do not belong to any individual.

It is a peculiarity of modern Western civilization to assign ownership to ideas. This corrupting transfer of notions of absolute private property from matter to mind reduces creativity to individual egos. As the poet Wendell Barry mused in a speech at the Jung Institute in San Francisco, "When my poetry is at its best, it is far better than anything I know about myself." Indeed, for much of Western history and in other cultures around the world, ideas could no more be owned than could earth, air, or water. It is essential to forgo such ownership if healthy change is to come about.

Credit, then, does not always go to the person who has come up with an idea. One must release one's ego from the need for acknowledgement so that those who are in the best political position to accomplish change may make the moves. This rule applies not only to legislative and political change, but also to business, professional and even domestic matters. Planners give away "their" ideas to those who have the clout to make things happen. In some cases, of course, planner and power may coincide, but even then, it is crucial that any new idea not be too closely identified with one person or department. *The more people there are in the system who think that they thought of an idea, the more leverage there will be for change.* As many people as possible should have a personal stake in the outcome.

In order to avoid polarization, plans for even sweeping changes are best presented in language that is neutral. New ideas should come dressed in old clothes. Gong words such as "socialized medicine" must be avoided so that opposition will not be mobilized. It may be very well—and soothing to the ego—to make principled and impassioned speeches in favor of justice, equity, and compassion, but *taking a stand* in this way, as the language implies, positions the speaker. Planners do not *stand;* instead, like yeast, they *percolate.* The formulation of new ideas in non-threatening language may not feel heroic, but it brings results.

Choice of the wrong words can block contact at the outset, as the following Sufi-type tale reveals.

Scientists from this world had positioned a satellite to broadcast a call to any passing interplanetary being, to show that there was intelligent life on Earth. The apparatus was linked by a translation computer which was designed to put the visitor's words or signals into English.

Sure enough, before very long a superior being on a space mission came across this device. Recognizing it, he dismounted from his ship and spoke into the apparatus. He said: 'Earthlings, I am a superman, out of Space. . . .' As the automatic translator began to type out this message, the scientists on Earth were hopping up and down in excitement. But the phrase 'Earthlings, I am a superman, out of Space . . .' was printed out, due to a lack of harmony between the vibrations of the two parties, as 'People of dirt, I am a virile heterosexual, without an apartment. . . .' So the message was interpreted as a hoax, because it was too trendy, and apparently nonsense, by the serious Earthmen. And the Spaceman: well, he was rather too serious-minded, too. He decided that as there was no reply the satellite must be broken, so he fed it to his space-cat.

The importance of the appropriate language to bring people together for change cannot be stressed too much. Verbal division between groups often conceals underlying agreement on many key issues. The planning entrepreneur works collegially; that is to say, planning for change is not imposed from above, as in a hierarchy, but is worked out pluralistically. In this model, groups who apparently disagree on the surface come together to reach change. The first task of the planner, then, is to help all participants see that the outcome need not be perceived as, "If I win, you lose; if you win, I lose." The planner tries to avoid gain-loss models, and instead strives to work with the common goals of all participants in order to bring all parties to a gain-gain outcome. Finding a language for these common goals is a key part of the planners' work.

Such principles can operate even in the smallest social systems, such as, for example, the family. A couple in crisis who comes for help to a family therapist may walk into the office in an intensely competitive and blaming frame of mind. Each party may believe that he or she is right and will be intent on proving the other partner wrong and in need of change. A skilled therapist will bring them to see their areas of agreement, which may simply take the form, "Things cannot continue as they are, because they are unendurable." The therapist will help the parties to see that they agree on certain essentials and will spend a good deal of energy at the beginning of therapy joining with the couple and helping them join with each other in a common commitment to change.

Once the circle of agreement has been drawn, the basis has been laid to expand into the outer circles of disagreement. When the couple gets into the old areas of conflict—and these may be Cold War battles that have hardened into rigid positions over the years and may even have become part of each partner's personal identity—the therapist gently reminds them of the fundamental agreement between them. Reference to the superordinate goal shared by all, that change must take place because the situation has become impossible, can often soften rigid stances and ancient polarizations. The therapist's attitude throughout this process is that both partners are right and no one is wrong. Old grievances are stated in neutral or positive language. Thus, the therapist may praise a blaming and critical spouse for taking such an active interest in the welfare of the family by constant vigilance. Or the therapist may acknowledge the hysteria of an intense and emotional partner as bringing expressiveness and excitement to the relationship. Paradoxically, such positive acknowledgement of embedded defensive patterns often serves change rather than stasis; once the pattern has been patted on the head, it can relax its vigilance. Strokes stoke change.

The same principles of respect and acknowledgement apply to larger systems as well. Hierarchical intervention imposes value systems and organizing concepts on others and forces them to act within a given pre-designed game. The collegial model, by contrast, initially acknowledges each participant's legitimacy and sets people to search for areas of commonality. When one has a variety of players of equal status, as in a family, a legislative system, certain corporations, or the United Nations, there can be no prior agreement to play the game that one group has chosen. However, such a pluralistic system does not represent chaos. Not all games, all views, and all organizing concepts disappear. Indeed, in such pluralistic systems there tend to be multiple agreements on a variety of sub-surface levels. The United Nations, for example, chooses a few languages around which discussions take place. In spite of political differences and international polarization, when the United Nations considers health, nuclear survival, or the needs of children, an underlying agreement on realities sometimes emerges. As in a troubled family, rhetorical squabbles may mask shared goals and common rules.

The planner must search then for those areas where a commonality of perceptions occurs and not expect—in spite of surface divisions—that all perceptions and goals are uncommon territory. Pluralism can conceal common interests. There are always shared organizing concepts that the participants cannot see.

The strategy for change, therefore, requires the full exploration of the common ground where individuals and groups agree to certain rules and can begin to extend their negotiations and their intense concern from there into the wider circle where rules are disputed or unknown. Collegial change requires a willingness to hear and express differences openly and non-territorially, always keeping in mind the core of agreement. Then the multiple perceptions and levels of concern about a given issue can be given a full airing. When participants learn to frame their discussions in the language of their "opponents," then the small areas of agreement about issues and rules can be extended.

The analogy of the computer may be useful to help understand this process of rules reframing. Those who work a computer soon find that they must learn the regulations and behavior set by the programmer or the computer refuses to work. This is a hierarchical model; the programmer sets rules, and the players must follow them. The programmer has all the power to design the game, so that those who wish to use a computer must agree to play the programmer's game. A collegial programming system would make each participant a programmer, and each one would learn the programs of the other players. We would enter a process of meta-games in which each system would receive acknowledgement. If health is defined as the ability to determine at least some of the rules by which one lives, then it is healthy for us all to learn to be programmers. Adjusting passively to another person's rules seldom feels quite right. *Homo ludens* has more fun making rules.

Youngsters who play the fantasy game Dungeons and Dragons, discover something similar. The children usually compete intensely to be gamemaster, because the gamemaster gets to establish not just superficial guidelines, but the very ground rules for reality, such as whether the country that one is playing has gravity or not, whether there are two sexes, or four, or five, what colors are visible in the spectrum, how many dimensions there are, and so forth.

As long as members of a society feel it imperative to buy into the existing game rules of the current ruling majority, then all the new players—the women or minorities moving into established organizations—have to learn a new game. They are, therefore, at a double disadvantage. Psychologically they are weakened because they must play by other people's rules and therefore feel powerless. Practically they must learn rules that are new, alien, and imposed from outside. These newcomers are judged by rules that have been created and practiced by those already in the club and are assessed by standards for which they may have little respect. But new players all bring their own rules and standards with them derived from their class, caste, minority status, and sex. In a collegial system, such rules can be incorporated.

This principle applies on all levels of social organization, from the politics of the street gang and the office through society as a whole. The game rules of the dominant American culture define the goals of life as wealth, power, and success. Although one can find spiritual pockets in this dominant materialistic ethos, little groups of people who seek community, salvation, or enlightenment, contemporary society is so obviously and overwhelmingly materialistic that it is almost tedious to speak about it. But we must remember that this dominant and pervasive materialism is JUST ANOTHER MAP. As drab and commonsensical as it may appear, it is not, as so many tough-minded business people seem to believe, any more the "real world" than is the communion rail or the poem.

This materialist map, and its unquestioned acceptance by the have-nots, the haves, and those moving in between these two statuses, impoverishes everyone's vision of human possibility in capitalist and socialist societies alike. All those on the way up have to learn a new game, the rules of which are already set, while the process leaves a tremendous number of powerless people incapable of coping with the rules. There are still a limited number of programmers. Many of these to be sure are new personnel, but the essential structure of the total game remains unchanged. Where there are strong and weak, haves and have-nots, where the system is built to cut up a pie of fixed available resources, then there will inevitably be an enormous number of powerless and anomic people who will be filled with pain and with symptomology of all kinds, including physical and mental disease, crime, addiction, and personal brutality.

Both Dungeons and Dragons and the computer reveal the potential for designing alternative games with different values. Here the issue would not be powerlessness, but collaborative effort to improve not just a piece of the organization but the total structure. Such a goal would mean the restoration of heterogeneity in values and rules, so that people throughout the society would no longer define themselves in terms of the often bankrupt values of the ruling majority. It would mean stimulating the creation of social forms in which greater numbers of people could be programmers or gamemasters. This model suggests that we can deal with powerlessness and disconnection by designing models in which individuals do not play established games. Such a change could improve the total harmony and balance of individuals, families, communities, socio-political systems, and the earth itself.

It is obviously tremendously difficult to achieve this. All change brings with it resistance, disturbance, and pain, not the chronic pain of the current game, the symptomology of powerlessness, but the chaotic, unpredictable pain humans experience when the rules of reality are shifting. People in all segments of the society can be expected to experience intense disturbance as old patterns are loosened. For the have-nots, this change means moving into the existing system and challenging it to change its rules and standards.

Such advocacy is painful—but it is also healthy. When social groups become involved in larger processes, when there is an atmosphere of action, hope, and the end of powerlessness, then some of the chronic symptoms of powerlessness—psychiatric breakdowns, midnight emergency room visits for "bad backs" and "sore throats," addiction, crime, and apathy—diminish.

Those of us who have observed the social search for alternative models of behavior, models that challenge the existing fixed-pie and shortage-of-resources models, are aware that such a search is painful indeed. Whether this search is conducted in communes, the retreat centers of the "new religions," families, schools, or community groups, the attempt challenges humans to their very foundations, and many who try give up. What is being suggested here is not an easy technical solution to the ills that afflict us, but a fundamental, urgent restructuring of our dominant values and social forms, undertaken independently in all the places where humans meet. One cannot even predict whether such an effort would succeed, or what the marks of success might be.

The challenge of such change is especially acute for those of us in the helping professions. No one can deny that those of us who are in the "change professions"—in medicine, planning, psychiatry, and social work—owe our very livelihood to the fact that there are powerless and unloved people who need our help. If the networks had not broken down, if people were not disconnected and fragmented and frustrated, there would be no jobs for the likes of us. Do we, then, *want* change? What will happen to our jobs? Do we have a vested interest in the perpetuation of lovelessness and powerlessness? We must examine our motives carefully, deeply, and thoroughly.

We in the helping professions need to look not only at our economic investment in the status quo, but also at our psychological stake. Are we ready to forgo the power kick we get when we impose our norms and values on those "less fortunate" than we? Can we confront and challenge our own values so that we do not continue to impose our own imperfect models on others? Revolution, we know, begins at home. We in the helping professions must bear witness with our bodies and minds to our commitments, commitments that include giving up our illusions that we can predict how change will take place or what the final consequences may be. This means giving up control. It means giving up being right.

Although such a model of change, when described in the abstract, sounds difficult and alien, there are in fact emerging forms within the professions that may offer us prototypes. In therapy, the old model in which the patient spent years of dependency (and thousands of dollars) in order to resolve internal conflict is gradually being replaced by a number of new, briefer, and apparently more effective methods. In many of these, the medical model of dependency has been abandoned, so that the relationship is no longer doctor-patient, but coach-client. This simple change of language carries a wealth of implications, for a client, unlike a patient, is not one-down, powerless, and dependent. Nor is a coach, unlike a doctor, godlike, superior, and above the fray. Both poles in the relationship have been changed. Family therapy coaches, far from being able to predict the exact course of therapy, stimulate the complex family system to deal with itself. They can observe the system and its repetitions so that they can intervene to suggest new moves and new plays, while having no fixed model of a desired outcome. They are not potters working on clay or mechanics on machines. They are *coaches,* stimulating living beings to bring out and express what is in them and between them. They stimulate, encourage, and cheer on, but they do *not* have control of the situation.

The image of the coach is, in fact, essential to comprehend the non-control model of change entrepreneurship being suggested here. Teams, families, executive committees, or legislative assemblies are all *alive and open systems,* webs within webs of complex, multiple, interlocking systems. A coach, therapist, or planner can interfere in these open systems, but this busybody must understand that he or she is competing with dozens of others who are intervening in these systems all the time. A skillful planning entrepreneur should be aware of as many of the other intervening systems as possible—this is an essential part of the map-making process described above—so that these other interferences can be taken into account. Good planners use the energy of these other interventions to move the situation in the direction of their vision. Their only advantage over the other intervenors is that they have mapped this open system and its interlocks before taking action and that they are committed to continue remapping as new information emerges in the unfolding situation.

Again, all this must sound very complex. If the social sciences and public planning had not emerged at a juncture in modern Western history when subject and object were radically separated, so that an active, "objective" agent worked on an inert, almost mechanical body, society, city, or school system, it would hardly be necessary to remind planners that they are not engineers. Planners are *active* in an *active* situation, a reality for which many planning paradigms do not account.

Coaches, then, cannot control the whole situation. The weather might have made the field wet or dry, the crowd will have a certain mood, the players will have relationships to each other and to multiple others outside the field—ailing parents, wives, husbands, friends, landlords, children, pets, insurance companies, and so forth—and the coaches as themselves have their own personal histories that they bring to the situation. Their scope of action within this intricate, alive, moving, unpredictable situation is relatively limited. But there is room to act, although the exact outcome may be difficult to discern. Coaches neither float passively on the surface of the situation nor cut ruthlessly and mechanically across it. They move with what they are given.

This idea sounds so absurdly, almost lunatically, simple that it hardly seems necessary to write it down. But, in fact, most planning has not been done this way, and because it has not, planners have been caught, again and again, surprised by the unintended consequences of their programs, whether they be urban renewal projects or corporate sales campaigns. The experienced planner knows that even with the most careful mapping and comprehensive futurology, that *the only guaranteed product of an action will be its unintended consequences.* Accepting this truism will take planners a long way toward abandoning their egocentric assumption that they control the situation. *No one* controls the situation.

Planners can, however, have a *direction* and can move themselves and others in it. This is perhaps best illustrated by a story that Lama Govinda likes to tell about the scope for skillful action. If one's goal is to cross a river, there are many ways to do this. The modern, Western image would be to engineer the crossing—to cut across all that is happening by building a bridge or using a motorboat—and thus violate the living fabric of the situation with multiple pollutants and alterations in tides, currents, water chemistry, and so forth. The unknown and unintended consequences of this engineering approach are enormous. Many Westerners, faced with criticism of such an approach, feel that the alternative is completely passive, to surrender all control of the situation and to float like a leaf on the water, hoping to reach the other side but lacking the ability to make intent effective. Lama Govinda, tells us that there is another way which is neither a passive "going with the flow" nor a violent cutting across it. In a canoe or a sailboat, one works with the other forces in a situation—wind, tide, and current—to cross the river. One uses all that is currently happening. One is active in a living situation.

The goal of the change entrepreneur, as we noted in the previous chapter, is to create major change in a crisis situation where most people are looking for a quick fix. Crises are the most opportune times for planning entrepreneurs to work. Part of their skill has to be a sense of timing. *During a crisis, the ordinary human resistance to change is softened, because the status quo has reached the point of unendurable discomfort.* People in pain seek change, but what they generally want is immediate relief such as splints, codeine, Valium, and other quick fixes. Even married couples who go for counseling in a state of crisis want relief from their suffering without having to change anything fundamental. Whether in a legislature or a private office, clever planners use this moment when they have been invited to intervene to introduce major, structural change, in addition to the band-aids and aspirins for which their clients are pleading.

The steps of this intervention are as follows. The planner introduces the new direction not as a blueprint, agenda, or plan, but as a *story*. The introduction is informal, tentative, imprecise, and imagistic. "What if we . . ." stories work because they do not mobilize opposition. They are fluid, evocative, and tantalizing, so that those who hear them can find their own interpretations. The story/plan can be many things to many people. Its very looseness allows alteration and transformation as it travels through the collegial system that will shape, pass, and implement it. In this poetry of planning, everyone gets to be a bard.

The following selections from the Sufi texts of Idries Shah explain better than I can the usefulness of stories.

No account of teaching-stories can be really useful unless there has been a recital of some of these tales without any explanation at all. This is because some of the effect can be prevented by an interpretation: and the difference between an exposition and a teaching-event is precisely that in the latter nobody knows what his or her reaction is supposed to be (from any doctrinal standpoint) so that there can be a private reaction and a personal absorption of the materials.

Eat Your Own Fruit

A disciple once complained, "You tell us stories, but you never reveal their meaning to us."

Said the master, "How would you like it if someone offered you fruit and masticated it before giving it to you?"

In fact, the plan as story probably corresponds more closely to reality than do the old blueprint models. The story recognizes that transformations can never be predicted accurately, nor unintended consequences avoided. How can the dying caterpillar in his depleted cocoon imagine what it will feel like to fly? How can a frog explain to a fish what air is like? One does not know until one gets there.

Once the story has been invented and started on its rounds, the entrepreneur needs to *sell the leadership,* in order to obtain legitimate authority and power to proceed. In therapy, this selling is called joining, and it is an essential part of change. There has to be some trust here and permission given to move freely.

Once the leadership has legitimized the entrepreneur, he or she begins preliminary mapping, the rough process of "casing the joint." Tentative leverage points are identified, allies with something to gain by working with the entrepreneurs are spotted, and power relationships are roughed out. This preliminary process depends very little on formal data and heavily on gossip, hearsay, feel, and on informal information networks. It is especially useful to identify ambitious newcomers who are not yet in power and for whom alliance with the planning entrepreneur could be an advantage. Floating the story and watching where and how it moves and changes is a useful way to do this preliminary mapping.

The story, now somewhat refined, is next prepared as a policy statement in the classical way, although with certain crucial differences. In order to keep as many participants as possible in the game, the story must be imprecise in detail, so as not to mobilize opposition. The goal is to keep all interested parties involved in the story-writing, so that they will continue to have a stake in its outcome. The multiple urgent needs of the various participants must be addressed in the story, while at the same time, major change—board game change—is also introduced in the policy statement without being heralded or emphasized. The plan satisfies as many immediate goals as possible, while *in toto* it redesigns the entire map. It does not *proclaim* that it does so. *Revolutionary change can occur in the absence of revolutionary rhetoric.*

Major change, then, is best brought about during moments of crisis. Such moments, affecting as they do all participants in a given system, make new alliances possible. This leads us to yet another rule. In the search for key leverage points to accomplish major change, *it is essential not to be hampered by standard notions of ideological opposition.* In developing the story and in bringing about major board game change, one must *approach old enemies.* They may be in as much crisis now as everyone else. It is crucial to develop coalitions between ancient opponents, between those who have been the victims and those victimizers who are now also in pain. This is the "Trickle Up" theory of social crisis, and it is when pain and crisis have trickled up to the top that the moment for major change is ripe. Timing is essential here.

Do not expect, then, that any group will be completely closed to change. In fact, those groups or individuals who are most resistant *must* be involved in the process of creating change, for several reasons. As noted already, inviting their participation in the early stages gives them a stake in the outcome. They will then perceive what is happening not as something being done *to* them and imposed from outside, but as a process in which they are active and have some control. In addition, the change entrepreneur needs to stimulate their resistance during the initial stages of story-floating. Resistance to change cannot be considered negative—the friction of resistance in fact heightens and sharpens and lends energy to the events. It is not to be suppressed, feared, and avoided. *There is no change without resistance.* Inviting resistance to be expressed early in the process allows issues to emerge that might help the entrepreneur anticipate the fallout of any reform. It is critical to involve those individuals who are most resistant, not only so that they may reap some rewards from the change, but also to invite them to commit themselves actively to the process. This will help enormously to ensure the long-run success of the change, for the fewer polarized outsiders there are, the better the chances are for the survival of a new way of doing things.

In inviting this collegial participation, the planner must be deeply committed to self-effacement. Falling in love with one's individual vision of a desired outcome will make collegial planning impossible. The planner must *give up control;* one who is not prepared to do this should not attempt collegial planning. The planner is not a mastermind, a trickster, or a magician who manipulates others into the *illusion* that they have a stake in the outcome of a given change. Instead, the planning entrepreneur creates a situation in which ancient enemies and polarized groups *actually* participate in change. This means, of course, that the content of a given plan cannot be predicted in advance. It will probably be far from an ideal model. The advantage, however, is that it will have a chance to work. Inviting participation at early stages can also reduce the volume of unintended consequences. By reducing polarization, this type of planning also facilitates implementation. The entire process, from beginning to end, has a kind of unity.

The planner, then, liberates creativity in all members of a given system. Trust is crucial here. In floating the story, planners need first to trust their own instincts. The initial phases of story creation and permeation throughout the system occur on multiple levels, of which the cognitive may be only a small part. Change may present itself, somewhat as ideas for poems or novels do, as a *seed,* an image, an insistent and often partial vision. This image needs to be trusted and allowed to live. If it is authentic, it will reverberate in those who hear it and this reverberation will stimulate further images and further development. Crises stimulate such unconscious acts of creation; a kind of healing poetry is released when conservative stasis is broken. One needs to be alert and open and aware during this seeding process, but calculations are not appropriate at this time and may deaden this essential creative process. Let the critic wait. The idea is to let something *new* emerge in the period of danger and opportunity that crisis allows. Cognition may be stale at such a time and positivist static may drown out the dim emerging music of new ideas.

Seeding the story prepares, then, for the future. While a bill is being written in a legislature, for example, a set of processes are set off that engage others not just for the act of creation, but for the implementation that must follow. A brilliant bill, a film scenario, or an architectural plan mean nothing at all if they are not carried out. On the other hand, change begins before implementation. Thoughts have lives of their own; simply gathering information and floating the story stimulate change. Therapists know that they intervene in a family system the moment they ask their initial, "What brings you here at this time?"

One could call this kind of change a Yoga for change, for it is essential that planning entrepreneurs, like therapists or yogis, be relaxed, open, and non-manipulative. Ideally, they are giving people the freedom to trust what is in them and to allow its emergence—and merging. They are truly coaches who encourage people to learn to change. Once, however, the therapist or planner takes sides or gets angry, frightened, or tight, the situation narrows and becomes rigid, and the process of creative emergence is blocked and stifled. The therapist and the planner create an atmosphere of trust in which people can bring out what is in them, but the therapist or planner must then be prepared to *hear* it. Recoil, judgement, disgust, disapproval, or fear all foster polarization, distrust, and a return to the old—and stagnant— way of doing things.

The plan, once it has been put together in this collegial way, is then ready to be put into effect, to be incorporated into legislation, administrative change, or changes in family communication patterns. The feedback process does not stop at this point. In fact, there is no clear *moment* when change *stops*. Follow-up is based on the assumption that the move made is not perfect, and that revision, monitoring, and new change will be the normal and natural sequel of reform. The planner must be alert to all the intended and unintended consequences that any major change entails. Because change normally is instituted in only one system among multiple interlocking systems, the planner must watch how the social learning stimulated by the change travels into these related systems. How does a change in health care delivery affect the schools? Economic development, housing, health, medicine, education, delivery of food services, all are interrelated. The gigantic map that these multiple interlocking systems represent can barely be comprehended and certainly cannot be controlled. But an intervention at any point in these systems affects all the other systems. Good planners watch to see how these changes move, so that they are always circling back to the initial map-making process. In some sense, mapping, intervention, the location of key leverage points, passage, implementation, and follow-up all occur simultaneously. They are not sequential. One moment contains all these processes at once.

V.

Health and Change

The great majority of us are required to live a life of constant, systematic duplicity. Your health is bound to be affected if, day after day, you say the opposite of what you feel, if you grovel before what you dislike and rejoice at what brings you nothing but misfortune. Our nervous system isn't just a fiction, it's part of our physical body, and our soul exists in space and is inside us, like the teeth in our mouth. It can't be forever violated with impunity.

Boris Pasternak
Doctor Zhivago, 1958

Why Health?

I have chosen health as the central metaphor or value around which this handbook for change entrepreneurship is organized for a number of reasons. In the first place, some central value is essential; we are discussing the quality of human life and the means to plan for its enhancement. Although this book is political, about power, about implementing change, it has a set of values at its core. It is written with the belief that there are many others in this world who share these values and would welcome guidelines, practical advice, a handbook of rules so that they could become more effective in seeing these values brought to life in these chaotic times. Ideas abound; the universities and public agencies and corporations around the world brim with creative, energetic people who would like to make an impact for the better while they live. But anyone who has tried to promote change knows the enormous journey, the Himalayan trek, from idea to action, from expressed value to concrete results. Most plans do not survive the climb, and many planners become discouraged. One of our purposes, then, is to "re-network" these often isolated and frustrated people, to let them know that they are not alone, and to encourage them to continue their efforts.

Health has been chosen, secondly, because it may be the toughest problem facing us worldwide. In America, for example, those who have worked in health planning, from the social services to the insurance companies, know that the American health delivery system, as it is called (and I will comment on this strange *health delivery* idea in a moment) is among the most daunting to challenge and change. The inertia and resistance to change in this burgeoning sphere of our lives is enormous, and the capacity of the medical establishment to resist reform is massive. In the richer portions of the globe, increasing billions are spent on medical care without anything like health being achieved, while in the Third and Fourth Worlds even the basic physical preconditions for health—food, shelter, and decent medical care—are chronically and tragically absent. Apart from the threat of nuclear holocaust (which is, of course, a question of health in its broadest meaning), the health of all of us is the most urgent problem facing humanity today. To assert that human health is our central value is to take on the most difficult, urgent, and resistant problem facing all of us. By focusing on health, where there has been so much hope and so much failure, we deliberately choose a tough subject.

Thirdly, health transcends ideology, and the divided contemporary world is in urgent need of such unifying metaphors. The quotation from *Doctor Zhivago* with which this chapter begins refers to post-revolutionary Russia, but it would ring a response in American corporate executives, tenure-seeking professors, bored school children, welfare recipients who are often forced to lie in order to survive, and millions of other alienated and dissatisfied people whose basic needs for meaning and purpose are violated by the systems in which they find themselves. Health does not come from outside of us, but it can be destroyed by outside forces. Where connection is absent, as in many parts of our fragmented cities and suburbs, or where connection entails the necessity to lie, as in Pasternak's Russia, our Western workplaces and schools, and even in our families, then pathology, *disease* ensues. If day after day we are compelled to say the opposite of what we feel (whether this be claiming sexual satisfaction in the bedroom in order to save a marriage, or voting for bills one does not approve in order to save a political career) then our souls are diminished and we are not healthy; we are no longer fully alive. The soul cannot be forever violated with impunity.

By asserting that the health of the soul is essential to our full aliveness, we are aware that we are challenging the materialist values that underlie health and social planning both in the capitalist and socialist countries as well as in much of the developing world. Health is not merely physical wellbeing. One can be full, fat, warm, and dry— and sick. To be healthy is to be fully alive—physically, mentally, spiritually, and emotionally—and to be connected in a fulfilling way with the natural and human world that surrounds one. In the large recent literature that has been inspired by the holistic health and self-care movements in the United States, it has been repeatedly stressed that health and medical care are separate and that health is not a *product,* nor can it be *delivered.* As Robert Hoke writes, "The phenomenon of health is a living activity, not a product. It is not something to *have,* but a way to *be.* It is a procession, not a possession." (*Potentials,* p. 107) Not even the most sophisticated high-technology medicine can "deliver" health, any more than a preacher can *deliver* faith or a spiritual master can *deliver* enlightenment. The more sophisticated physicians in the Western medical world show an awareness of their limits, and tend to describe themselves as medical technicians rather than as healers. But too many of them still write and talk and lobby as if the delivery of ever more sophisticated (and expensive) medical services is the only route to health, as if adequate medical care and health were synonymous. "If the only tool you have is a hammer," Abraham Maslow writes, "you tend to see every problem as a nail." (*Potentials,* p. 101) And so the American medical establishment hammers away at the delicate living fabric of our human and natural systems, often with the best will in the world.

This is not, however, an attack on the profession of medicine as practiced in America. I hope to address those in the profession who have struggled with the issues of health and planning and have engaged in the recent discourse about the nature of health. To identify enemies, villains, opponents would violate the healing purposes of this book. I am aware that a physician, any individual, caught up in the politics of a hospital or a county medical society may, like Pasternak's protagonist, be constrained to say the opposite of what is felt day after day. Systems tend to develop their own lives and imperatives, and this is why one can talk about institutional learning, social learning. But no system is completely homeostatic, completely closed. It is at the point that the medical system opens to, connects with other systems that surround it (and this is not one point, but multiple, multiple places) that there is some flexibility and hope for change. And, of course, such change is already taking place in a number of ways. But I will discuss these hopeful signs later.

In addition, I wish to note that in choosing health as my central value, I am not addressing questions of medical care alone. Health is not the province of any profession. My primary concern is with the entrepreneurship of change, and with locating a central value that can unify disparate interests and activities. I choose health because it seems to do so, but I am not primarily concerned, then, with the reform of the medical system in any part of the world. My goals are broader than that.

It would be possible to write a book about planning entrepreneurship using the idea of justice, or equity, or participatory democracy as the central value and, in fact, books have been written around these themes. Many of these concepts, however, evoke associations that many peoples in the world associate with Western bourgeois democracy, and in their evocation, can lead to polarization. Health is a more neutral and universal value. It can encompass both the Marxist notion of alienated labor, Eastern ideas of the necessary unity of subject and object, and the Western liberal freedoms of the individual as embodied in the first ten amendments to the U.S. Constitution, and the United Nations declarations of human rights. Health is a capacious and non-polarizing image. It rings a common response in those who might find themselves otherwise ideologically polarized.

In addition to its capaciousness, the idea of health is specific, urgent, concrete, and immediate to us all. In order to activate large groups of people for change, they must be touched where their urgent concerns are. We all want, at least on the conscious level, to be healthy. Whether we are old people facing limited budgets and declining physical and mental capacities, young parents worried about our children, or sexually active singles worried about AIDS, we all think about health every day, with every bite we eat and every step we take. Should we cut down salt? Does peanut butter cause cancer? Can meditation lower my blood pressure? Should I get more exercise? What can I do about my chronic feelings of restlessness and depression? Will putting my aged mother in a nursing home kill her? We all face these and similar questions every day. The idea of health, then, contacts each of us at the most concrete, mundane, and immediate daily level and expands from there into the entire universe.

What is Health?

Medical care is specifically concerned with a defined set of difficulties, symptoms, or illnesses that require treatment and rehabilitation—and, ideally, prevention as well. Health, on the other hand, is the normal process of growth and development that includes the biological, psychological, social, and spiritual issues in human individual and social life. With our increasing understanding of the interconnectedness of the earth's systems and the ecological nature of all activities, we now realize that the so-called system that affects our health has enlarged to the totality of the planet. Even medical care, that subsystem of health, does not exist in isolation. Disease care in the United States today accounts for almost ten percent of the Gross National Product, and its impact on all the other social systems is ever-increasing. Hospitals affect the economy and the traffic patterns of the neighborhoods and cities in which they are located, medical insurance payments and expenses consume an ever-greater proportion of corporate and union budgets, while the crisis in the government-sponsored health programs for the needy and the aged have elicited nationwide attention.

Health, then is not a special commodity. It is not something that can be bought and delivered, or produced by physicians. Health is related to life, how we are created, grow, live and die. It is how we are and how we feel, as well as how we relate to those around us, both our intimates at work and home and the many others whom we encounter more or less casually. A brief encounter with a tailgater or a rude salesperson can affect how we feel for hours. Seeing a dead dog on the highway, reading a disturbing newspaper story, enjoying a plum tree in bloom—all these acts affect our health. Health is related to the total environment in which we live, including all the living organisms that make up our world.

It is almost as if the living organism most relevant to us is the earth, and each of us is a living part of that alive being. As with many living organisms, the whole can be healthy while a piece is sick or dying, and yet the sick piece affects the whole. And if the whole becomes sick and dying, each part dies with it. But on this planet, things are occurring with such speed and with such major significance, we seem to have lost control of the situation. Our first job, then, is to reassign responsibility for health back to the broader community. This is not a new idea; the ancients understood it well. The shaman faced with illness dealt both with the ill person and with the community. As the shaman moved the ill part, the whole community was engaged in coming together, joining their energies in a variety of activities that regenerated the whole and healed the part at one and the same time.

As most physicians would be the first to admit, they are no longer priest-healers, or shamans in this sense—although the old-fashioned country doctor of current nostalgia may have been somewhat closer to a healer—so that the achievement of health cannot be left to the professional medical community. To expect the best of medical care— and in many ways it is superb—to deal with health is to ask the physician to intervene in the whole community as well as with the patient. Such, indeed, was the goal of medicine when the profession in its modern form took shape in the early nineteenth century, as the quotation from the French physician, Virchow, bears witness. Virchow wrote, "Should medicine ever fulfill its great ends, it must enter into the larger political and social life of our time; it must indicate the barriers which obstruct the normal completion of the life cycle and remove them" (Duhl, *Healthy Social Change*, p. 141). Virchow voiced the ambitions and hopes of the great European medical faculties as they took shape in the nineteenth century. Faced with increasing secularization—the abandonment of religious constraints and ethics— migrations to the cities that tore millions away from their integrating villages and customs, social dislocation, social fear, rising crime rates, massive illegitimacy rates, infanticide, prostitution, and urban unrest and revolution, the medical faculties set themselves the task of healing this new society by the scientific understanding and management of human society. It was this impulse that fostered the new public health movement which formed in Paris in the 1820s, the beginnings of modern urban planning, and the attempt to find a secular basis for the existence of the human family, which was seen as the protector of infants and women and the civilizer of men. This was the heroic age of medicine; its ambitions and hopes were unlimited. That it only partially succeeded may have been due to the limits of its vision. It failed to take into account the spiritual, the irrational, the inexpressible, what we would call the right brain, and what the phrenologists who were active at the time would have celebrated as the superior activities of the forebrain. In fact, the new professionals who fathered contemporary medicine located these right brain activities in the "primitive" brain at the rear of the skull and asserted that lesser breeds, the non-dominant classes, such as women and the darker races, were unfortunately dominated by this primitive, pre-rational brain and could thus never take on the responsibilities of rulership.

We are all still, to some extent, influenced by this Victorian medical and professional legacy. It is partially to stimulate those who are active in public policy to transcend the limits of this time-and-culture-bound image that this book is being written.

Our current task, then, is to examine the differences between the medical model of change, which has served most social planners until now, and a new health model of change that planners should adopt in order to plan for the complex future. Medical care focuses on a defined and limited set of difficulties, symptoms, or illnesses that require specific care. Health, as we have indicated, is far more than this. When health coping and adaptation fails during stress of crisis, dis-ease results. Disease can bring social, physical, psychological, or spiritual "illness" or often a confluence of two or more kinds of illness. While clinical medical treatment often deals with specific disorders mechanically and in relative isolation, an interdependent notion of healing seeks to return the whole individual to an optimal state of well-being and growth. Health reintegrates and reconnects.

We now know that although there are some normal, generally determined processes of development, the path to health varies by culture and society. Even the very definition of health is socially constructed, as references to nineteenth-century medicine should make clear (Duhl, *Healthy Social Change;* p. 39 for references). Rational social planners, the inheritors of nineteenth-century positivism, have not always or even often taken this diversity of cultural or ethnic pathways and norms into account. They have tended to assume that all healthy development was essentially the same and that goals and norms were similar whether one was Black, Caucasian, American Indian, male, or female.

In addition to these cultural compexities, we must recognize that people who live in heterogeneous societies find it more difficult to achieve health than those who live in homogeneous societies. The crisis that spurred the development of the nineteenth-century public health and urban planning movements was fueled by the widespread destruction of the homogeneous villages of European peasant society and the massive social pathology that ensued. The same process still occurs around the world. But it is not merely in the crisis of transition from a homogeneous to a heterogeneous society that health is threatened. Merely living in a heterogeneous society poses its own problems, as people find that they need specialized skills, must market their labor, and often live in multiple, conflicting worlds. As those who have been invisible to the majority culture emerge into visibility, stress increases for individuals, for institutions, and in policy itself. (Duhl, HSC, p. 39) The achievement of health may be particularly acute for minorities within a dominant culture, for women (and the erosion of the female sub-culture is one of the constants of modernization), for racial minorities, and for small ethnic groups. When the attempt to achieve healthy development breaks down under stress and crisis, the disease that occurs often takes a particular form. Typically, disease and the form it takes depend upon the predominant culture. Minorities in heterogeneous societies are, in consequence, often alienated from their own traditional cultural definitions of disease and health. Even the definition of their symptoms reflects their alienation.

Which European philosopher first proclaimed that nature is dead? We have talked about the earth as a living organism of which we are all living limbs, but are we being any more than sentimental? The sad truth is that most of us are trying to achieve personal and social health in an environment that is man-made. Our natural environment, if such there ever was (and even Neolithic hunters inflicted incredible damage on the vast herds of ungulates in the European plains, apparently driving several species to extinction), has been supplanted by a man-made environment that seems at least as uncontrollable, so that much of our disease is both man-made and difficult to cure. Does the present high incidence of drug abuse, alcoholism, mental illness, and suicide reflect an epidemic of individual illnesses, even failings, or is it a product of particular social, man-made conditions? If these diseases are neither completely individual nor completely social in origin and course, so, on the other hand, is health, too, a synthesis of the individual's internal environment with the entire external environment—physical, social, spiritual, man-made, and natural (Lalonde, 1974).

Talking about health in a heterogeneous society becomes, then, very complex, for health derives from the totality of existence and not just from internal experience. It is our belief that health is in all of us, from the moment of conception. The DNA molecules and the genetic templates they lay down do not limit our growth and health, but offer broad ranges of possibilities; but from the very moment of conception, that potentiality of aliveness becomes more and more limited.

The environment—the uterus, the mother, what she eats, how she feels, the birth experience, the family, the community, and the world—these provide the necessary setting for our survival, but at the same time, they impinge, assault, and limit us. Our capacity for aliveness is slowly stunted.

What are these assaults? They come about through adverse nutrition, and from limiting environments, a teenage mother's uterus, a cramped city apartment, isolation from social networks, no contact with the natural world. These assaults also come iatrogenically; the very things we often do to prevent, treat, or educate leave a mark or scar on us, and deform us in some way. A premature baby might be saved by oxygen only to suffer lifelong blindness as a consequence of this treatment. Preservatives to prevent spoilage in food might damage fetal development. But the assaults of the environment are most often not due to medical iatrogenesis, but rather to the very quality of the life we assume.

Parents, with the best will in the world, often educate children to reproduce themselves, and thus bleach out the aliveness of fresh creativity. All institutions, from the family to the school, are governed by the imperatives of the past, but health is an optimization of aliveness in relation to a current, present, living environment. More than that, health means synthesizing that contact into a way of life.

The work of Hans Selye on stress is suggestive at this point. Selye argues that when the body can no longer count on its resources to cope with assaults and stress from the environment, then it breaks down at its weakest points. Too much stress from the environment almost guarantees illness (Duhl, HSC 81)

What brings the body-mind the ability to cope with the environment? Apparently, the most important single variable here is the ability to command events that control our lives. This is true on the individual as well as the social level. Whether this be through meeting basic needs of love, security, or nutrition, or through skills learned through education (both formal schooling and informal social learning), or through the ability of the community to respond to what is really needed by the signal of illness or pain, the result will be a direction toward health.

Growth and learning must be whole and not fragmented. It has been all too easy to focus down on issues or discrete parts that we can manage or understand. In doing so we have separated ourselves into fragments. Schools teach cognition, families and peers teach feelings. Sports programs manage the physical, poetry is off in the language departments where it will not touch too many with its disturbing, fresh visions; the churches get what is left of religious and spiritual awareness; and sexual development is assaulted by the media, by peer pressure, and by the pill. How rarely are all these tied together into a whole.

Our fragmented bodies reflect our fragmented social institutions.

Experts from multiple institutions connect with, teach, or treat the bits and pieces of our divided being; dentists get the teeth, but move over half an inch to the throat, and it is a drive across town to the ears, nose, throat specialist; manicurists get our fingernails, but the dermatologists, plastic surgeons, health food stores and the mass media compete for our skin; and when it is the soul or mind at issue, our choices from among competing therapies, spiritual traditions, biofeedback techniques, and counselors are bewilderingly immense. There seems to be no one out there, no person, no institution, to connect our whole body-mind-soul to a whole universe. There is fragmentation within and without. Divided selves, we confront a divided world. And yet one ancient definition of health is that it represents a synthesis of both the internal environment of the individual and the broader external environment which is physical, psychological, social, and spiritual.

Fragmentation on the individual level is matched by disarray on the institutional level. We have increasingly fragmented the solutions to our problems so that each expert has taken on specific turf responsibilities and there are few who function as networkers, to integrate and pull together the diverse groups that are involved in dealing with any particular problem. For example, in a recent study in the state of California, it was demonstrated that the fragmentation of services to children is such that one of the only solutions may be to abolish each specifically defined, isolated service, and start anew with a comprehensive, holistic one that deals with children and families. It would not take a study to convince the social workers, psychologists, and other officials who try to help children through this maze, and for whom frustrating hours are wasted on the phone as they try to penetrate the Byzantine bureaucratic complexities in order to find help for their clients. These institutions are in disarray not because they are staffed by individuals of bad will (although this is the first, Kafkaesque impression) but because these institutions grew up, in an uncoordinated fashion, to deal with the problems of the past. The disarray in health and social service institutions is paralleled by institutional crises in many other fields: in economic, political, governmental, and other spheres.

Let us then speculate about the meaning of health in this complex world. For, in spite of its heterogeneity, in spite of our contemporary fragmentation, we still live in a universe that is connected, in which every thought and action affects the whole. Health, then may mean the ability to choose the appropriate reality or the appropriate dream depending on the issue that needs to be faced. Thus, we need not choose between our left-brain functions of rational, analytic, precise thinking and the imprecise, intuitive, and subtle answers that come out of our insights derived from religious and spiritual states. The synthesis of internal and external environments, in such an attitude of choice, is altered; in fact, the barrier between inside and outside becomes somewhat flexible and transparent. We are not faced with either/or choices. To adopt the metaphor of the hologram, it is possible that by searching thoroughly within, we transcend narcissism and egoism and connect with all that is without, all space and time.

There may even be laws that could describe such mystical-sounding unities. But with our limited knowledge, we can at least design open systems that allow and respect the simultaneity of internal and external paths to health. Health may indeed be the utilization by individuals as part of a communal society of all their senses, even those beyond the ones we normally recognize. We need not adopt difficult or alien spiritual stances in order to make this possible in our society; all we need to do is to design systems that do not *stifle* this possibility, allow the choice of this dream, this reality, for the times and people who can explore and benefit from it. What we need is to go beyond the illusion of technique, and to move beyond the idea that health can be *produced* by technique, external, rational knowledge, and control.

Jonas Salk applies the biologist's law to the S-shaped curve to our planet-wide dilemma. Salk sees the growth of bacteria and viruses on agar plates as a metaphor for the world's situation. At a certain point, as the bacteria multiply, the nutrients on the plate are no longer capable of sustaining the growth of the population, so that the S-shaped curve shifts from experiential growth toward a plateau, or no growth. Salk draws the parallel with our situation, arguing that our institutions, like the nutrients on the plate, are no longer capable of sustaining their ability to deal effectively with our problems. When the middle of the S-shaped curve shifts from experiential growth toward a plateau, Salk argues that a transition is required into a new epoch, one that Salk calls Epoch B, where the metalanguage, the way one conceptualizes issues, becomes markedly different. We are all, to one degree or another, inept, because we are products of a way of thinking that emerged in the previous epoch. We need to begin to see ourselves and our problems as taking place in the midst of the profoundly unsettling transition from Epoch A to Epoch B. A paradigm shift is needed to deal with this crisis—but this does not mean that we need begin to see our situation only in terms of shortages, and ever-tighter controls of our diminishing resources and exhausted institutions. To see our situation only in terms of shortages is to see it in the conceptual framework of the old epoch, Epoch A, the period of growth.

As we move from Epoch A to Epoch B we are faced with a need for alternative models, because the first temptation, as we confront the existential and social deprivation of this transition, is to emphasize increasingly sophisticated controls over both environment and people. In this crisis, however, we may have an alternative choice: to accept a completely different set of metavalues. The metavalues of planning based upon collaboration and of health seen as wellness rather than disease control could lead us to learn to live more wisely.

For those who hang on to their conceptual frameworks and institutional loyalties as learned in Epoch A as we move to Epoch B, the transition seems terrifying. Where there was plenty, now is scarcity; where there was hope, no longer hope. We have no shortage of handwringers and doom-sayers among us as we confront the future.

But the path is not linear, single, without choices. At every moment, there are multiple choices. It has been said, for example, that crowding causes disease. But even *crowding* is socially constructed. Crowding in cultures where their governance permits coping and adapting does not necessarily lead to the same pathology as does crowding in populations who have no skills or coping ability. There is no single, material reality imposing a single, historical course of deprivation upon us. Our choices of reality are there at any moment.

To adapt, then, to change as time changes, is a process of social learning. We need to develop new images, new conceptions, new ways of seeing what is happening so that we avoid feelings of helplessness, terror, competitiveness, and the discouraged conviction, held worldwide except by the very rich, that "the party's over." As we face our diminishing resources, we must learn that even the idea of a "resource" is socially constructed, and that we may have available to us resources yet unimagined. This new learning will require our full creative energy, our full aliveness. As Arthur Koestler has written, "Every creative act involves . . . a new innocence of perception, liberated from the cataract of accepted belief" *(The Sleepwalkers).* The routinized, technical safety of our old planning programs, the control model, has shown that it cannot cope with changes as massive as our planet is undergoing. Our old ways of seeing things are like cataracts, films over the eye that prevent our fresh perceptions and fresh creativity as we pass through this time of crisis. The sense of control that the old ways give us, the security, is illusory. But even as we shed these illusions, the next step need not be fear and despair, but a liberation of human and institutional creative energy to meet this emergency.

It will not be easy for the creative—it seems that it never is. Creative children, for example, have been shown to be too disruptive because they do not fit into the organized curriculum of classrooms. Creative adults in institutions confront similar problems. Institutional adaptation as well as personal adaptation is essential if we are to survive and fulfill our potentials as members of a society in a state of flux. The way of life that has heretofore been only for the alive and the healthy must begin to be developed across the board, even if it appears that survival itself—survival of humanity—is the goal. To conserve what we really have requires adaptive potential by individuals and society.

Health, then, is not a fixed state, nor can we set out its precise content. Because it is not fixed, not homeostatic, it cannot be defined as a goal, a place, to be reached with certain actions. Health may be defined as creativity or aliveness, but both of these terms, it should be noted, describe, not states of being, but processes, and somewhat difficult processes to define at that. Health is an attempt to get ready for a new state and development. Health, in the current world-wide emergency, may be seen as the release of self-healing energy under crisis stress. Health is the *movement* toward health.

When people are sick, they should first be met on the level of illness where they can first deal with the specific damage, then return to earlier issues and make a jump toward aliveness. The same is true for society as a whole. In our current crises, we need to deal both with the flagrant symptoms and with the more fundamental conceptual restructuring described above.

This takes us back to the medical model of health described above. We are not suggesting that this model be thrown out in favor of alternative healing and integrating systems. In our striving toward health, we need to make choices—and to have choices available—so that we may seek the appropriate method, the appropriate reality, if you will, freely. This means that we need to have available to us many ways of thinking about health, many conceptual structures, and many systems of application from which to choose or to apply simultaneously.

For the purposes of discussion, we will describe three such approaches to health.

The first is the familiar medical model, the clinical treatment of illness and accident that dominates Western countries and that has become immensely influential, powerful, and wealthy in the nineteenth and especially the twentieth centuries. On the whole, this system has focused on making people *Notsick;* it has concentrated its enormously effective and intricate technology on diagnosis and treatment of illness, physical, and mental defects such as birth disorders, and accidents such as burns, breaks, and gashes. Its goals are limited, and most physicians count their treatments successful when symptoms are alleviated or eliminated. Although the public still turns to the medical professions for healing, most physicians recognize that they are not healers but medical technicians, experts who are trained to diagnose disorders and apply the appropriate technology to relieve illness and pain. That is to say, modern medicine has developed by and large without a model of what it is to be a healthy human being. Health, for most physicians, if they think about it at all, simply means the absence of blatant symptomology.

This medical model has extended itself into areas such as obstetrics and psychiatry where its limits have, in recent years, become most visible. What technology is appropriate for a spiritual crisis? What violence is done to the birth process when the laboring woman is hospitalized, defined as a patient—as ill—and subjected to the often inappropriate application of the massive technology of birth? Is it enough to define birth only in terms of products—a symptom-free baby and mother? So much has been written in recent years about the limits and the dangers of the medical model when it is applied to birth, death, and consciousness that I will not belabor these questions here. But it is significant that many physicians now recognize that clinical medicine is silent when confronted with the fundamental human dilemmas, the meaning of birth and death and full aliveness. There are profound limits to what even the most sophisticated science and technology can do here, and when they are misapplied, they hurt mothers, babies, the troubled, and the dying.

Nevertheless, modern clinical medicine, applied appropriately, has made millions of us gratefully *Notsick.* It is only where medicine has colonized fields in which its techniques create more iatrogenesis than benefit that it has done such dramatic damage, and it is to these spheres that many of the lively recent attacks on the medical profession have been directed.

Finally, it should be said that Western clinical medicine, although it has focused on treatment, has not ignored prevention, and that recent developments in American and Swedish medicine have brought preventative medicine more to the center of the physician's activity. Prenatal care is preventative, as is your physician's yearly advice to stop smoking and get more exercise, but now preventative medicine has been institutionalized in such innovative institutions as health maintenance organizations. Even with this new emphasis, however, prevention within traditional Western medicine still means simply that— *prevention* of symptoms rather than attainment of well-being.

The second major approach to health is public health, an outgrowth of Western medicine that began in the early nineteenth century in Europe and has had a strong impact in the United States and in recent years in programs in the developing countries sponsored by the United Nations and other international organizations. Public health programs of nonclinical disease prevention are familiar to us all in epidemiological studies of patterns of illness, of industrial poisoning, of the effects of food additives and fertilizers, and of other factors in the environment that cause disease or other symptomology. But although public health agencies deal with the environment, they, like clinical medicine, do so on the whole in order to relieve symptoms in the population. Public health, like clinical medicine, has as its goal the prevention or alleviation of illness and accident rather than working toward a goal or model of health, well-being, full aliveness. Public health originated in a rational, secular, materialist, right-brain culture, so that while it draws important connections between poverty and crime, between stress and alcoholism or emotional disorders, its material substructure limits it conceptually. Its excellent programs may not fulfill the human hunger to be healed, where healing means a full integration of the physical, the mental, and the spiritual, where healing means inner and outer peace and balance.

This brings us to the third approach to health, one which I call the public's health. Activities in this sphere do not directly bear on illness and its prevention, and yet there has been a growing awareness in recent years that these activities affect our health in the broadest sense of the word. Here we mean health not merely in the terms of survival— a relatively symptom-free existence—but in the terms of full aliveness. The distinction between surviving and full living is drawn from the work and publications of the Peckham Center in London, where, for over a generation, the health of the constituency of this community center was recorded and studied. The Peckham people described this constituency as of three types: the living, the surviving, and the dying. The twenty to twenty-five percent of the population who were described as dying included those with serious mental and physical pathologies, that is, those who were more sick than well. The sixty-five or so percent of survivors included those who get along and who go along, who are relatively symptom free, who adapt to the status quo. Are these lives of quiet desperation? Or simply of chronic, low-grade malaise? In many cases, survivors may be quite contented. Not everyone enjoys risk and change. The third and smallest category the Peckham people designated as the fully alive, the risk-takers, challengers, non-adapters, those who are unafraid of disorganization, awkwardness, and change. Clinical medicine and public health have brought their clients to survival level, but on the whole, neither they, nor the other institutions of modern Western society such as the school or the corporation, have fostered full aliveness, optimum health. The fully alive can be irritating and unpredictable; because they do not live within the yesterday's rules of our institutions, they can threaten or disturb those survivors who do.

It is possible to imagine that in other times and other ways of living on the earth, there were more people in a given group who attained to full aliveness, that, for example, a Native American in pre-conquest days might have lived more days of full aliveness in his perhaps thirty-year lifespan than a modern American businessman in his 72.3 years or a modern Swedish nurse in her 78.9 allotted span of years. It is possible, too, that such thoughts are merely romantic speculations; we can never really know, but we do dream, and dreaming is what full health may be about, to dream and to have the scope to act in service of the dream. We can imagine, from our fragmented, separated institutions and selves what it is to live another way.

The public's health, considered in this sense, bears no direct relationship to illness and its prevention. It is connected with every human activity, from the nature of the work experience, to political action, to the availability or lack of availability of networks and of arenas in which individuals and groups can exercise the ability to command the events that affect their lives. The public's health depends on much more than clean water, toxic-free air, inoculations, exercise, abstinence from cigarettes, and an adequate diet. But if health is, as we have argued, derived from the totality of existence, what can any individual or agency do to promote health?

The public's health depends on the ability to command events that affect one's life. It depends on access to multiple realities, flexibility, and choice rather than rigid and antiquated programs. The health of the individual depends also on context—on the nature of the community in which people find themselves. (In a recent study of child abuse, for example, two communities were studied—a community with a high rate of abuse, and one with a low rate. The crucial variable was found to be, not race or class or economic status or unemployment rate, but the quality of community life, the degree of connection and trust between neighbors and the existence of community institutions in which people could come together.) The public's health may depend on the ability to see the stars at night or to smell earth turned, on access to outdoor space, flowing water in its natural state, the sky, trees. We all sense that this may be so, although proof is lacking. Health may depend on constructing transportation systems in which people can walk from place to place rather than riding. Part of our nostalgia and regret for the destroyed hunting and gathering societies that existed in parts of the world until the nineteenth and twentieth centuries comes from our sense that the men and women and children in these societies lived in intimate contact with nature and in daily celebration of the sacred, in an enchanted forest that lost its enchantment when trees and rocks and water became commodities, and when human labor and even art became part of the market.

As we undergo the transition from Epoch A to Epoch B we seem to be nearing the end of the commodified society. As we confront our shrinking material resources, now may be the time to redefine our goals, realities, and ways of life, to reintegrate the alternative realities that have been shoved aside in the era of material progress. This may not be the time for the more effective use of mere survival strategies, not as individuals and not as a society. It seems to be true that the move to full aliveness does not come with the improvement or refurbishment of old models, the coping methods of Epoch A, but a more fundamental change in our entire ways of thinking, feeling, and acting. Modern chemistry tells us that organization does not arise out of previous organization, but out of disorganization, chaos. Do we have the courage to face, on a society-wide level, the dark night of the soul from which true aliveness may spring? It may not be the survivors who become truly alive, but the sick. In the ancient language of religion, rebirth follows death, a dying of some sort. Hanging on with survival strategies may preclude the move to full aliveness.

We now find ourselves in a social crisis world-wide of major proportions. The Chinese language tells us that crisis has two components: danger and opportunity. We do not minimize the dangers of the current transition, nor do we adopt apocalyptic language lightly or out of boredom or frustration. But there are signs worldwide that mere muddling through, gradual, incremental change within the old systems and organization no longer works and may actually do damage. Fundamental change is terrifying, but it may be our only choice. There are times when mere survival strategies no longer suffice. I will discuss these signs and vision of change within the new model of health I have put forth here in the next chapter.

VI.

Healthy City

I have argued that many programs for change are as fragmented as the problems they face because they deny the relationship to the whole. We must conceptualize problems in their totality, and not merely address a fragment. Most programs in their "dream" lack the sense of the whole and the awareness that people are unavoidably connected to each other and to the full environment, the entire planet, the universe.

But if we think globally, can we act at all? What do we do before we become enlightened? "*Act* enlightened," advises the spiritual teacher. Very well, but how do we do that? Some of us must continue to try to act globally; the ecosphere demands it. Could, for example, a world-wide ecology watch made up of representatives from communist and capitalist governments and industries act in time to save us from the predicted greenhouse catastrophe? Can we take steps so that our ocean of air and our oceans of water survive the by-products of our technological age with which we are transforming and perhaps ruining them? Organizations such as *World-Watch* act on the planetary level. In national and state government and in nationally-based private organizations such as Common Cause and the Sierra Club there are also ample arenas for action on the global scale.

What is needed, however, is intervention on multiple levels. The planet is large. Effective, visible action is often on the local scale. Where local action is planet-wide, momentous change is possible. Because of the ways we live, the city is the local arena for most of us in the late twentieth century.

The importance of the city as a habitat for humans is underlined by our knowledge that by the year 2000 the urban population of the world will exceed three billion people and that almost 50 percent of these city dwellers will live in cities which have populations of over one million.

Local action in cities must be undertaken with knowledge of global interdependence and its impact on cities. The healthy city is part not only of a living regional community, but of an interdependent, living, planetary community of water, air, forests, and animals. It is also part of a larger human community in which the policies and decisions of other cities, nations, and international corporations that function outside a city's borders may dramatically affect a city's prospects for health and survival (quoted from Global Education Associates letter of 2/28/86). Walled cities that can shut out external forces are found only in history books, and even these medieval fortresses were not shut off from the surrounding environment. Global interdependence has increased to the point that local action must always be undertaken with a planet-wide vision. At the same time, in the midst of growing planetary consciousness and interdependence there is a commensurate need for a sense of identity rooted in a particular place. How can cities play a role in providing a sense of identity while also involved in the global interactions of an increasingly complex and interdependent world?

In eighteenth-century France the jurist and *philosophe* Montesquieu argued a failing case for the continued existence of intermediate bodies between the individual and the central government in order to temper the monarchical tendency toward tyranny. His view did not prevail, and those provincial assemblies, lawcourts, and other local bodies not already destroyed by the Bourbon kings were finished off by the thorough and rational revolutionaries of the so-called moderate phase of the French Revolution. Even at the time, conservatives such as the Englishman Edmund Burke protested that the living body of a society and government cannot be so violated without dire consequences. (The spectacular unintended consequences of this piece of social planning culminated with the Napoleonic dictatorship and a France devastated by years of war.) It is to the organic metaphor evoked by Burke, applied to the modern city, that we turn for our final chapter.

Burke and Montesquieu were aristocrats who used the corporative social metaphor in order to defend privilege. This ancient organic image, beloved by conservatives since the beginning of political philosophy, can also, however, be rich in implications for those who wish to promote change. The idea of the body has altered over time so that when moderns describe a city as an organism, this image resonates with different meanings for us than it carried for the Greeks or the Scholastic philosophers or the Conservatives of the nineteenth century. Specifically, our model of the body is far less hierarchical and less mechanistic than theirs were—it reminds us not of a peasant population made up of flesh and bone which is dominated by a royal head, but of an interdependent, redundant, communicating system in which memories reside in muscles and decisions can be made by the feet. Modern biologists also describe the body as an open system, one that is constantly taking in, giving out, and changing in response to its surroundings. Finally, its redundancy makes it "cost-inefficient." If one nerve pathway is destroyed, another can be developed. This redundancy gives the body great resiliency in the face of stress or trauma. A healthy body is constantly learning and changing.

A healthy city shares the same living qualities a healthy body has. It has open communication pathways, non-hierarchical governance, the ability to adapt to stress, redundancy, and the capacity to learn and change. And each city, like each living creature, is unique. Physically, socially, and historically, it is not quite like any other being or place. Healthy cities, like healthy people, are in touch with their pasts. Identity is created over time. Like organisms, cities pass through developmental stages, either changing and adapting, or withering and dying. Some cities are older than Abraham; Rome's lifespan, for example, has been immense, and it has gone through cycle upon cycle of change. In the present environmental context of any city—as with any organism—inhere many possible futures and many pathways to failure or success.

The model of the healthy city, then, is of a complex systemic organism that must create continuing and dynamic means to cope with both its internal problems and with its connections to the outside world. Cities in which people prosper and thrive are complex, multi-dimensional communities that have, not a single purpose or a single industry, but rather which meet the total and varied needs of heterogeneous populations. The healthy city, like the healthy person or family, also has clear boundaries while it is open to the environment. Healthy cities and healthy individuals have both identity and permeability; they synthesize the internal and external environments. When the parts work together with balance, flexibility, and harmony, when the organism can respond to stress and resolve conflict, then the city is healthy.

It seems that the concept of a healthy city is one that is understood intuitively by many people. It is one of those phrases that somehow says a great deal with very little explanation, has people nodding in agreement, becoming interested, enthusiastic, even excited. These are the reactions we have found among politicians, planners, public health professionals and many others as we have discussed the idea in Europe, North America and Asia. At this point, however, the concept is only beginning to take shape, and no doubt it will assume a somewhat different form in each city, just as each living thing is unique. The city is an obvious starting point in discussing and working for both better health and a better society. For it is in the cities that life's drama is acted out. In the industrialized world today, most of us are conceived, born, grow, develop, live, love, have and rear our children, work, play, grow old and die in the city. The city is the crucible of human experience, human development and human health. It is the vital centre of our industrialized world, a site of creativity and innovation. City government is the level of government closest to people, and often has most, if not all, of the resources that are necessary to enhance health without resort to higher levels of government. We are intrigued by what it is that makes the city and its people healthy, and what the potential may be to enhance or promote that healthfulness.

We believe that our health and the health, perhaps even the very survival, of our species requires that our cities provide for us the opportunities and the environments necessary for us to grow and develop, to achieve our full potential in a mutually supportive and non-exploitative manner, without impairing the stability of the ecosystem upon which our health and survival ultimately rests. A healthy city is thus much more than one that has good health care services and a population with high health status. Our focus is not just upon the health of the population, conventionally defined, important though that may be. For the health of a city is crucially dependent upon how well the city functions as a physical and social environment; to what extent and how well the city provides the community resources that people need not just for health in the conventional sense, but to develop to their maximum potential; and the degree to which the city makes it possible for people to mutually support each other in growing, developing and performing all the functions of life.

Of course, each city is unique, having its own history, its own values and its own concepts of health and progress. On our part, our values are clear. For individuals, to summarize what I wrote in ch. II above, they include the right to full growth and development, the provision of basic needs and a life of peace and freedom from fear. The principle of human rights also includes personal freedom and some control over the events that affect one's life. On the group and community level, our values favor creating ways for people to work together without exploitation, finding a glue of trust, cooperation and respect, so that communities may be formed that do minimal violence to individuals. On the global level, we are concerned with fair distribution of the earth's resources, an ecological awareness of the limitations and fragility of our planet, and the absence of violence between peoples.

These values, of course, are not new, startling or even controversial. In one form or another, they have been repeatedly endorsed at the United Nations and in the statements of many other global forums such as the World Health Organization, UNICEF and UNESCO. The challenge that faces the city is how to put these values into practice so as to achieve health.

The Urban Context

We live in an urbanized age. In 1850, no society could be called urbanized, yet by 1925 48% of the European population and 54% of the North American population lived in urban localities. By 1975, these figures had reached 67% and 77% respectively, and by 2025 the great majority—88% of Europe and 93% of North America—will live in urban places. Similarly the USSR, while only 18% urbanized in 1925, had reached 61% by 1975 and was projected to reach 87% by 2025 (Pacione, 1981, Table 1.1).

Thus anyone interested in improving human health and well-being in the industrialized world must necessarily be concerned with the state of health of the cities and their people. This has been explicitly recognized by the European Region of WHO in establishing the "Healthy Cities" project that seeks to enhance the health of cities by supporting cities and their people in the development of initiatives and processes promotive of health.

Yet some question the city's ability to initiate and implement health initiatives in the face of a variety of problems that include deterioration of the physical environment, poverty, unemployment, economic stagnation, homelessness, hunger, family violence, crime and youth alienation. In some respects, cities may be seen as the potential or actual "victims" of national and international policies—most spectacularly in connection with the threat of nuclear annihilation, more mundanely as a result of social, economic, immigration and other policies.

On the other hand, others point to the many real strengths of the city. For instance, it is in the city that the greatest variety of skills, resources and talents are available; it is the cities, Jane Jacobs (1984) argues, that are the economic powerhouses of nations; it is in the cities that invention, the arts and other forms of creativity have traditionally flourished. Furthermore, city governments are often the closest level of government to people that have the mandate, the authority and the administrative resources needed to bring together the wide variety of skills and resources needed for a multi-sectoral approach to health.

What do we mean when we talk of "the city"? As Phillips and LeGates (1981, 82) point out, the concept of the city does not inspire consensus: "There is no precise definition of the word 'city' that social scientists or anyone else can agree upon." At one level, the city is a collection of buildings and roads and their associated transportation, communication, water and sewage systems—the hard infrastructure. However, this is more a description of an archaeological site than a city. Clearly, a city is more than simply bricks and mortar. A city has a life of its own, it has a soul, a spirit, a personality. Writers such as Jan Morris, the travel expert, have eloquently portrayed the persona, the living nature, of each city (1985).

Historically, the city may have begun as a centre of trade, because of its strategic location on a main transportation route, or because of the religious and symbolic nature of the site. Either way, cities frequently had enormous religious symbolism, what Lynch (1981) refers to as the "cosmic city", one that negates time, decay, death and fearful chaos, Yeats's Byzantium. Such a city was based upon order, stability and dominance, with religion and faith as the core of the city. That religious and spiritual significance is seldom found today, its place taken, perhaps, by Mammon and his temples, the bank headquarters. But the role of spiritual or mythic symbol remains an important part of a city's identity.

Phillips and LeGates (1981) suggest that the common elements that describe a city are permanent residents, a large population living at high density and a heterogeneous population. However, there are no criteria delimiting how large, how dense or how varied a city can be. To an economist, a city is a place "where the local inhabitants satisfy an economically substantial part of their daily wants in the local market" (Weber, 1921). To an anthropologist, it may be that a city exists "only when there are cultural ingredients considered essential to urban life—the fine arts, exact science and, in particular, writing" (Phillips and LeGates, 1981, 83). A sociologist, of course, would focus upon the interactions between the inhabitants of the city, and for her or him that would be the city. It is these interactions that Duhl (1985a) terms the "soft infrastructure" of the city:

> It is the geography and history of the city, with its varied populations, their immigration patterns and cultures and their art, music and poetry that govern the city. These characteristics and events, interacting with the still broader context of region, state, nation and world in all their manifestations, determine how people are born, live and die. The laws, taxes, regulations, business practices and the availability of infrastructure emerge out of the political struggles of all these groups and people.

To a political scientist, a city is a legally and politically defined entity with clear boundaries and jurisdictions, with a mandate, authority and powers usually defined and limited by a higher level of government. To others, a city is a place where the maximum number of transactions take place (Meier, 1962). Clearly, what the city is depends upon who you are and how you perceive:

> Researchers now believe that subjective reality is every bit as important to understanding and fostering successful urban life as the concrete and asphalt of objective measurement. . . . How people actually perceive their environment is as important as the environments themselves (Goleman, 1985, 11, 14).

We should keep in mind the words of the late Constantine Doxiadis, one of the most provocative thinkers and writers on the topic of the city. According to Doxiadis, our image of the city has gone through a number of phases in the past four decades, from buildings to transportation, then to society and now to nature and energy:

> . . . we know that in fact people all over the world suffer from much more complex situations than these fashionable attitudes would have us believe, we must not allow passing fashions and incomplete diagnoses to divert us from understanding the real problems or basic diseases of human settlements, and their causes (Doxiadis, 1977, 50).

We believe that if we are to come to grips with the complex reality of the city, it is perhaps best understood holistically, as an organic, living system, partly organism, partly ecosystem. As an organism it is composed of a number of subsystems—arteries to transport materials and nutrition, nerves to carry messages, an excretory system, a respiratory system—and like an organism it must learn from its mistakes, adapt to and cope with change, repair itself and communicate and exchange with its fellows. As an ecosystem—"a functioning interaction system of living organisms and their effective environment, physical, biological and cultural" (Berry and Kasarda, 1977, 16)—it is composed of a variety of competing and cooperating groups in a state of dynamic balance. Its strength lies in its diversity, its interdependence, in the efficient use of energy and the continuing recycling of material (Lynch, 1981). Of course, the city is really a social ecosystem, and a direct analogy to a biologic ecosystem may be misleading. But, clearly the city is a particularly important subsystem level in understanding the human ecosystem and the concept of the city as a human ecosystem is a popular one.

Scale affects the nature of a city's patterned life. The informal and unwritten rules of village life do not suffice as a city grows larger and becomes heterogeneous. Formal rules such as laws and regulations as well as formal agencies of enforcement become necessary. Waste removal can no longer be an individual affair. Traffic needs to be regulated. The infrastructure of roads and bridges needs maintenance. Money has to be collected to pay the inspectors and enforcers and maintainers of this infrastructure. All this is obvious.

As scale increases interdependence and complexity, there is a need for an increasing number of rules of the game, both formal laws and informal cultural patterns of behavior. And here the possibility arises that those with power—those who get to the rule-makers and enforcers—can demand through a variety of means that others conform to their standards, even when such standards conflict with the dominant culture of the subject group. Native American children were once punished in the Indian boarding schools for speaking their mother tongues. Left-handed children were once forced to be "normal." Therapists "cured" homosexuality. Recently in San Francisco the Park Department arrested several Southeast Asians who were trapping squirrels and pigeons to meet their food needs. "This behavior is not done in the U.S.A.!" Conformity and adaptation were demanded. Such top-down dominance, when it becomes excessive, impairs the health of the organism, just as the human body suffers when the mind and will—the head—do not respect or heed the complex messages from the entire organism.

A city is a complex organism which, if you stretch this metaphor by comparing it to the human, has many organs and connecting parts. What makes each of us humans work is a complex biological and psychological set of processes that are able to perform different kinds of functions. Each part has within it a set of functions that are unique, and within each part are materials and mechanisms that assist in connecting it to the surrounding organs in the human organism. Think, then, of the city as having a heart and blood vessels, lungs with a respiratory system, a brain and central nervous system, a liver and metabolic system, and kidneys with an excretory system. These organs or systems with their functions could be compared to the energy, environmental, transportation, communications, nutritional, and disposal systems of the city—the hard infrastructure. There are also the connectors and a complex of interlinked organ systems of various kinds, the roads, the communications networks that carry nourishment and waste as well as messages to the other parts so that either the other parts can act in concert or the total organism as a whole can work coherently. There is no action that takes place in one part of the human organism that does not affect the entire person. So it is with the city.

Organisms learn how to be over time. Institutions when they are healthy also learn how to be and how to continue to learn. This capacity for social learning gets built into the city's invisible infrastructure—its culture, laws, business and social practices, the rituals with which it celebrates its past and plans its future, and the communication webs that link its disparate parts. Often an outside observer can see the repeated patterns that make up a city's personality more accurately than residents can. Jan Morris, a travel writer, is especially perceptive in picking up these subtle characteristics very quickly. Real estate agents and brokers often know the living body and mind of a city—its moods, its illnesses, its possible futures—better than the planners at city hall know it. Realtors are, for one thing, unhampered by the theory and the language of the social sciences.

Because the city is an open system, it is vulnerable to changes in the wider world. American cities in the 1980s—and to some extent, cities in other parts of the world as well—are suddenly being asked to take on responsibilities that the central government has performed for generations. Reagan's "New Federalism" is just one aspect of a worldwide trend toward decentralization. The American retrenchment from national responsibility for the welfare and health of citizens, a responsibility carried by the federal government at least since the New Deal, finds echoes in Canada, England, and other western industrialized nations as well. Even Sweden is reviewing its commitment to the wraparound state. Reagan hailed this policy as a return to the concepts that informed early American domestic policy—local control, state sovereignty, and power and responsibility returned to individuals and small groups.

Reagan seemed to believe with Montesquieu and Burke that intermediate bodies are best suited to perform many functions once assumed by the central government. Of course, it is possible that Reagan's rhetoric about local control was an ideological cover to enable his greedy plutocrat buddies to abandon responsibility for oppressed and helpless citizens so that they have more for themselves. Certainly the safety net has gaping holes. But even if this is true, the crisis caused by the federal abdication of responsibility for citizen welfare, has created opportunity. The return of local control may truly be an opportunity to revive and expand communitarian ideals on a human scale. Local control of programs must, however, be accompanied by local means to generate resources necessary to foster community health. Right now, the money is not there, but if communities have the will, resources can be generated.

The "healthy" cities, those with the capacity to respond to stress, are best suited to meet the crisis of decentralization and reassume their ancient functions as nurturers of their citizens. What then, are the characteristics of the healthy city?

The Concept of a Healthy City

If there is a widespread difference of opinion as to what constitutes a city, then we must expect an even wider difference of opinion as to what it is that we mean by "a healthy city." Some, of course, would argue that to talk of a healthy city is in itself a contradiction in terms:

> As a central thesis, I would argue that American cities are unhealthy places in which to live, work, play or visit (Kennedy, 1977, 9).
> The city is a centre of human illness and death. It is a place of concentration, exchange and diffusion of germs and poverty. As the place of possible cures, it creates illness; as the last hope of the hopeless, it is the citadel of death. The richer the society and the more dominant the city within it, the more these truths hold (Greer, 1983, 7).

Of course, not all observers of the city would agree:

> [Hinkle] suggests that the conventional view that modern urban societies are unhealthy for humans is quite contrary to some of the available evidence (Hinkle, 1977, 5–6).

The various measures we use to evaluate the health status indicate that since the turn of the century urban mortality and morbidity rates have been decreasing faster than their rural counterparts. Today, the big city advantage exists not only in the objective indices but also in people's perceptions. Cities are perceived not only to have better health care but also to have healthier residents (Palen and Johnson, 1983, 47).

As should be clear by now, when we talk of a healthy city, we do not simply mean one that has a low death rate or good hospitals, important though those might be. Mortality is not the only—probably not even the best—measure of health, given our current concepts of health, while we have already pointed to the fact that hospitals and sick care services are not the most important determinants of health.

Nor is a healthy city simply one that has good housing and a clean, safe, hygienic environment, though that too is important.

. . . within wide limits, it is not the physical condition of the house, neighborhood or human settlement that determines a person's health so much as his [sic] own social background, his perception of his environment, his relationship to other people around him and to his social group (Hinkle, 1977, 301).

We are, in any case, talking about more than the health of the people of the city, because the health of a city is much more than simply the health of its population. To an economist such as Jane Jacobs, for example, a healthy city might be one that replaces imports in a positive frenzy of creativity and innovation (Jacobs, 1984), while to an urban planner a healthy city may be one that has good physical characteristics such as housing, transportation and green space; to a sociologist, a healthy city may be one that promotes social cohesion, while to an educator it may be one that enables people to grow and develop; for an epidemiologist a healthy city may be one with high health status, for a health care planner it may be one that has high quality, accessible hospital and medical services, while for WHO it may be one that promotes health for all, enabling the attainment by all citizens of a level of health that will permit them to lead a socially and economically productive life. And for the person in the street, a healthy city may be one that enables them to make a living, keep a roof over their heads and food in their stomach, provide for their family, meet their friends, move around safely and, in general, to freely carry out all the functions of life. Each one of us understands the concept a little differently, according to our own interests and training, our culture and our values.

Nor can the health of a city be simply expressed in a set of facts, for there is a quality to the city that we must somehow capture.

> We are not looking for data that can be manipulated and arranged so that all the parts add up to 100. We are looking for understanding. . . . In urban diagnosis the observer looks for patterns, breaks in the patterns and deviations from the norm (Jacobs, 82–83).

Thus a healthy city cannot be described by tables of data and stacks of computer printout alone. It must be experienced, and we must develop and incorporate into our assessment of the health of a city a variety of unconventional, intuitive and holistic measures to supplement the hard data. Indeed, unless data are turned into stories that can be understood by all, they are not effective in any process of change, either political or administrative. For that very reason, we must learn to look at cities through the eyes of writers such as Jan Morris (1985), whose brief portraits of cities convey a quality and an atmosphere—an impression of the "health" of the city—that cannot be conveyed in any other manner. And we must learn to speak of cities as simply and elegantly as James Rouse, developer of the "new town" of Columbia, Maryland, when he asked his designers and planners to build him "a garden to grow people in."

It should be evident from the above discussion that the concept of a healthy city is a very broad one, incorporating ideas from sociology, urban geography, city planning, ecology, politics, economics, philosophy and a host of other disciplines in addition to public health. And, of course, the concept will mean different things to different people from different cultures, from different cities, even from within the same city. For that reason, our definition of a healthy city is one that focuses upon a process that creates the possibility of health for its people (however defined) rather than pointing to an end state. Our working definition is as follows:

> A healthy city is one that is continually creating and improving those physical and social environments and expanding those community resources which enable people to mutually support each other in performing all the functions of life and in developing to their maximum potential.

The challenge we face is twofold: can we find some broadly agreed upon dimensions that will describe a healthy city, and even more importantly, can we suggest processes that will enhance a city's health, and thus the health of its people.

First of all, healthy cities have a sense of history to which their citizens relate and upon which their commonly held values are grounded. In Toronto, for example, the Anglo-Saxon tradition, characterized by the British system of governance, represents the commonly held set of values and historic presence. Until the 1950s Toronto was a small, non-cosmopolitan town with a strong British presence. Despite the vast influx of immigrants from different cultures, the old British values have maintained their cultural dominance. Newcomers learn them as they arrive in the city. These norms include the British-Canadian concept of a benevolent sovereignty based on government as collaborative and cooperative rather than as individualistic, competitive, hierarchical, and divisive. The British-Canadian vision of peace, order, and good government coupled with respect for the Queen as sovereign, create an atmosphere for government in Canada that is in sharp contrast with the American experience. Where British values dominate in Canada, there is support for the government and for a common, government-provided infrastructure.

In Montreal, by contrast, the distinct French and English historical traditions and value systems make the picture more complex. The French-speaking Montreal residents, regarded until a generation ago as the "white niggers of the North," are acutely aware of their history and enjoy a lively and original culture. Because the Francophones have endured generations of discrimination as the only large French-speaking population in North America, they have had no problems in seeing their uniqueness and in preserving their culture and values in a sea of surrounding sameness. Martin Lubin (1985) has noted that this particular and paradoxical status of the Francophones has transformed them into adept and effective politicians. They have learned to "live in the cracks"—asserting themselves at politically correct and opportune moments. The genesis of the Quebec separatist movement is a case study in competent minority group behavior. A sense of history is immensely important to the Quebecois as reflected in a potent slogan on their automobile license plates which heralds: *Je me souviens* ("I remember"). They remember the discrimination and humiliation, but even more importantly, they remember that they are French and that being French means to have a distinct political, social and cultural history.

The values associated with the French culture are very different from those of the English. The Quebecois are decidedly social democrats. Thus, rather than a fee-for-service health care system as in British Columbia, Quebec has a capitated, socialized health care system. In terms of helping, charity, and social responsibility, in Quebec a person can be charged with a felony for *not* helping someone in a life-threatening situation, whereas in the English tradition, that same individual can be charged with a felony *for* helping a distressed person if it is determined that the help somehow aggravated the situation. Obviously the English and French values, traditions, and histories are quite different in the province of Quebec, although there is a common thread that distinguishes both French and British Canadians from many Americans. Whether in Francophone social democracy or Anglophone benevolent sovereignty, there is support for *community* responsibility for the health and welfare of citizens that contrasts sharply with some of the excesses of American competitive individualism.

It is possible, then, for a healthy city to be culturally diverse and yet provide historically grounded values that in spite of surface diversity, have some unifying threads. This leads us to the second characteristic of healthy cities. Healthy cities are multidimensional, age-differentiated and have a complex and interactive economy. Again, as with common values and history, Toronto meets this second criterion for health. The population mix includes Anglos, Italians, Poles, Greeks, Portuguese, Caribbeans, Latin Americans, Southeast Asians, and Chinese. The dispersion of people in downtown Toronto includes families, single people, the elderly, and the young. The economy is diverse, so that if one kind of industry or business fails, there are others in place to keep the economy stimulated. As the headquarters for most Canadian companies, Toronto is part of a world-wide economic web. Toronto is also redundant. Redundancy is not necessarily a valued quality in an efficiency-oriented model of governance, but it is an essential element in a healthy, multi-dimensional city. For a city to accommodate diversity of culture, race and age it must, like the human body, have redundant systems. Redundancy accommodates diversity, and it also provides backup systems during stress or failure.

Thirdly, healthy cities strive for decentralization of power and citizen participation in making decisions about policy. Like the body, the healthy city is not hierarchical. It is not a machine-like system ruled by a bossy ghost located somewhere vaguely in the head. We now know that a healthy body is a complex interactive system in which power and decision-making are decentralized. In the body, this decentralization works when communication networks remain open, that is when the circulatory and nervous systems function in a healthy manner. In the body, as in cities, there can be conflict between the central government and local control, between head and heart, or between exhausted muscles and a determined will. When the body's neighborhoods are ignored for too long, they protest with sprains or infarctions, or the communication networks become fouled, as in high blood pressure or nervous disorders, or the entire system can become lethargic and depressed.

Toronto has structured its city management to include citizen participation. Many city departments have sub-groups whose work it is to help people organize to make demands. This structure is especially effective in public health and in the school board. The next condition for healthy cities makes most of the preceding ones possible. Heterogeneity, multi-dimensionality, and dispersed sovereignty are possible only when there is some unifying theme.

To change our metaphor of the city from a body to a game, the healthy city needs a common gameboard for decision-making. The rules of the game need to be universally recognized and accepted by the players. There needs also to be a way to make meta-statements about the rules; all significant players should be able to comment upon and modify the rules when appropriate. And finally, the formal and informal rules, the overt and covert means of getting things accomplished, should not be too different.

Toronto works because although it is ethnically diverse, the people and the neighborhoods work together using common rules. In Toronto, the rules on the whole are British rules of communication and decision making, but they can be used by non-British Torontans in order to express and work for their needs.

Healthy cities are represented by leadership that focuses on the whole of a city and can visualize both parts and wholes simultaneously. Although this point would appear to be obvious, it is nevertheless an indispensable precondition for city health, and one that is by no means always realized.

Again, Toronto excels in this virtue. The leaders in this city serve not only their various constituencies, but also keep the total city and its context in mind. The phrase "beyond health care" and the concept of a healthy city originated at a conference in Toronto in 1984. The phrase means that the major means of improving health lie beyond the realm of traditional health care policy, and that the health of individuals and the community are best served when citizens participate in governance. The *polis* is healthy when all parts of it are active. Beyond health repeats on the level of the community what takes place in yoga or bioenergetics when the head "gets in touch" with the body so that balance is restored in the organism. The whole city, like the whole body, becomes more healthy, vital, and alive when the entire organism is awake and communicating, when leadership and body are in touch.

Healthy cities can also adapt to change, cope with breakdown, repair themselves, and learn from their own experience and that of other cities. Here, as well, the organic metaphor is useful. The city, like the body, can be seen as a living organism that must be flexible and must continue to change with circumstances in order to survive. The way in which a city responds as an open system to the world polity and economy may determine its survival as a healthy city. Oakland began its move from urban decay to health by adapting to changes in worldwide shipping so that it built a port that could handle container cargo shipping while its glamorous neighbor, San Francisco, held on to the old ways and lost the business. Ships now steam past the abandoned San Francisco ports to a revitalized Oakland, a city that adapted and changed.

Finally, healthy cities are those which support and maintain their infrastructures. The hard infrastructure of roads, sewers, water systems, services for children, the handicapped, and the elderly, recreational facilities, police and fire protection, are the obvious hard parts of the infrastructure that need maintenance. But healthy cities also need to protect and maintain the soft infrastructure—the common language, rules, values, history, and communication networks that make the *polis* cohere and give it boundaries. Here community rituals by which a city celebrates itself and evokes its past nurture this infrastructure. Boston, for example, involves the artists, businessmen, churches, musical groups, and so on in its First Night celebration every December 31. Originally planned to give Bostonians a healthy alternative to a drunken New Year's feast, First Night has become a beloved yearly ritual for almost a million Bostonians to come into the streets each year to celebrate their city and the day. Crowds walk from concert to church service to fireworks display in a jolly if chilly yearly reaffirmation of community. Planning for the event—like planning for a Sarvodaya workday in Sri Lanka—is as important for the community as the day itself and works to keep the invisible communication networks alive. First Night has spread to a number of cities, and San Francisco plans its first one at this writing.

Examples of Healthy Cities

Consider the Peckham Health Center in London, a pre-National Health Service center, a community "settlement" house where the focus on health encouraged and supported recreation, education, eating, group activities, and problem solving for individuals and community. This center was a place for families to gather, to learn arts and crafts, swim, or create a solution to the area's housing needs. Participation in community endeavors, in a healthy environment without medical care, was shown to improve individual and family health. Despite this, this center, although dedicated to health in all its manifestations, disappeared when health insurance and medical care were felt to be the answer for health.

"Settlement houses" have, in the last century, also been places in the city that concerned themselves with aiding in the resettlement and new learning of in-migrants to the cities.

There are the Danish folk schools that educate on all levels, not bound by what more formal educators consider official education. Where most schools focus on curricula outlined by "experts," these schools respond to the expectations of their students. If they believe they need a class on fish net repair, they get it. If learning how to take care of tools is the issue, classes emerge. Shakespeare may fit into a history class. Other classes mix culture with history and personal need.

The spread of such schools and those like them have mobilized communities. The Highlander folk school which educated farmers, workers, and community people in formerly segregated areas of the southern United States has led to generations of community leaders for the public good.

Some programs for disturbed youth have, under the leadership of people like George Lyward of Great Britain, created places where education, therapy, self help, music and arts, as well as mutual aid are mixed into a program that is labeled only as Finchden Manor, and not as a school, detention program, or volunteer group.

Community work groups for young people in the eastern European countries have combined community need, belonging to a group, and education in competence as part of their social programs. Highways, parks, and other needed places have been created while young people have formed an identity for themselves and an identification with their community.

There is the story of the adolescents of Budapest who "adopt" the public transportation buses and take care of them. By doing this they learn to repair them, and this responsibility has given their lives a strong sense of purpose. Independently, this idea was implemented in Oakland, California, by the transit authority in response to damage and destruction of the buses by youth gangs. These gangs were hired to care for buses and to see that no damage occurred. The problem has been reduced markedly.

There are the handicapped and their needs. The Centers of Independent Living, staffed and run by the handicapped in Berkeley, California, have developed full community programs to meet this population's diverse needs of living without loss of dignity or control over their own lives. Where formerly isolated and dependent, these handicapped are now a political power, playing roles in the political decision making not just in Berkeley, but in the communities of North America. This group has gone from isolation to participation in the community.

There are the new towns of Scandinavia, Great Britain, the United States and elsewhere, where the totality of human needs have been considered. Some of these cities are working quite well. Where cities have one function or goal, like the capital cities in the United States, Pakistan, Brazil, Australia, Canada, and some European cities, they have been less successful. Cities whose purpose is only governmental functions, as cities just for business—including the many "downtowns" of cities throughout the world—are social and human failures.

Consider the many models of comprehensive communities reflecting the concept of the American developer James Rouse, "a garden to grow people in." Success was in the conception and implementation of social and physical infrastructures rather than just the construction of buildings and roads. Open space, the use of bicycle paths that do not cross streets, and neighborhood development help create the social environment for a successful city. In Columbia, Maryland, Rouse even created the means for the first residents to operate with a governance structure that led to the eventual city government itself, which functioned as the community developed. Sadly, the architects of these new towns do not, themselves, live in them. They prefer the organically developed old towns. What is reflected is two-fold. No one group can design the vehicle. Out of the relationship of people living and working together new forms can emerge.

In and around Mexico City there are the people made poor by the oil crisis and the devalued peso who organized an "underground economy" of barter and mutual aid since they could not buy the things they needed and wanted. Here the "wants" became secondary to the mutually supportive relationships that allowed life to go on to a higher level than expected given the economic decline of the larger society. With the emergence of the underground economies in Italy and elsewhere are similar stories of community-wide mutual aid and support.

There is a Moslem and Sufi teaching that puts "reciprocal maintenance," our taking care of each other and our environment, as the highest human spiritual value—much in the way the Sarvodaya movement in Sri Lanka manifests the Buddhist cosmologies.

People in the Basque region who created the Mondragon cooperative took cooperative concepts and created a manufacturing activity which supports its people in many ways in a large area. Similar cooperatives in India, revolving around the need to produce and distribute milk, have grown to community organizations that deal with housing, farming, education, and health.

Alone and isolated, people have no networks although supportive relationships are central to all our needs. Hotels for single parents in Denmark sparked a similar homelike housing project in Denver where housing is not the only goal. In the Denver setting, education, development of job skills, child care, nutrition, and health services are put together within a program of learning how to cope with the world.

Cooperative relationships can be learned, as in Kenya where people from various fields—bankers, truckers, bicycle repair persons, storekeepers, and government bureaucrats—are brought together, and learn together, rather than in their specialized groups. When we learn our jobs separately we do not understand the interconnectedness necessary to get things done. Asians and other cultures with large, strong family relationships know this well. It is this "soft infrastructure" that communities need, something we too often forget in our love of modern technology.

In St. Paul, Minnesota, a mayor used planning a common steam plant with a network of pipes to heat downtown and the poor area as a means to get the various factions in the city to talk with each other where before there was either no awareness or tension.

Communitywide case managing for frail elderly people has turned into community development in San Francisco. Where certain of these old people formerly required nursing home care or hospitalization, a communitywide program, On Lok, now serves them in their own homes, assisting in the provision of care, food, and other necessities without their having to deal with the diversity of agencies that exist.

The horror of Acquired Immune Deficiency Syndrome (AIDS) in San Francisco has been transformed from a medical problem where death was the only outcome to a communitywide support program where volunteers, political groups, and the general population is making the AIDS problem a model for the social means to deal with catastrophic illness. Again, it has been the creation of a broad social infrastructure by all people concerned with the situation that made the difference.

In the City of London, the now-abolished County Council gave funds for new programs and activities to innovative groups in order to stimulate social entrepreneurship. By encouraging diversity and new activities they believed they could stimulate the development of a city that would meet the needs of its ever increasingly diverse population. There are people concerned with development and alternative technologies that are appropriate to the true needs of people.

In San Francisco and Detroit there are the community mediation programs that assist and teach people to solve their own problems without resort to police, courts, official agencies, or doctors. Categorical agencies are only partial solutions. Mediation by peers can cut down the use of services by encouraging people to solve their own problems. Many of the problems sent to mental health clinics or the courts could be resolved in the community.

There are community nutrition and family planning programs in Thailand that connect to broader community development. Other organizations have strong and deep concerns about alcohol and drunk driving, the needs of the developmentally disabled, with improving transit for non-business purposes, bringing vendors into marketplaces, cemetery upkeep, theatre and culture, and much more. There are even the Chinese consultants who place buildings in correct relationship to the energies of the earth using geomancy, a way of understanding that is foreign to most of us, but which works for some.

In summary, if one turns not to the professionals, who stay within their own fields, or to the volunteers alone, we can create a larger community concern for issues. These larger "gameboards" of politics are not what we usually call politics. Despite our propensity for specialization, it is the gathering within the city of people concerned with the interconnected issues who are connected.

I have cited case studies of cities which have, by luck or purpose, become "healthy." But how can the planner work to foster health where it does not exist? How can a city in crisis use the danger and opportunity to promote health? How can a "depressed" city wake up, as Oakland has begun to do? How can a fragmented and disconnected urban mess recreate boundaries, identity, coherence, and common rules?

Handbook for Creating a Healthy City

First of all, respond simultaneously to the immediate crisis and the underlying causes. The patient with a tension headache needs both aspirin for the immediate pain, as well as longer-term therapy such as marriage counseling or body work to deal with the underlying causes of the tension.

In addition, involve all parties from every possible segment of the community in the solution. This stimulates health in at least two ways. The more people who participate in a decision, the more limited the backlash. And also, participation *in itself* fosters health. Local control can have meaning in terms of personal and social health. If a policy is locally generated, not mandated by an agency in a distant capital city, those who participate have the health-giving experience of controlling the circumstances that affect their lives. We need to recognize the importance of decentralizing the responsibility to those who are most affected by the policy. This means that the expert has to LET GO of power and control.

Any attempt by cities to develop a "healthy city strategy" requires commitment, involvement and participation at three levels: Commitment of municipal (and where appropriate, regional or national) governments; involvement of a broad-based coalition/network of community agencies, organizations and groups; and participation by citizens.

Therefore, I recommend the creation of community *round tables*. This concept of round tables is an idea that has been around for a long time. Although often used in international meetings, round tables seem to have been all but forgotten in our American cities in recent years. Many businesses hold round tables as do a few cities, for example Seattle and Redondo Beach, California, but such meetings are largely piecemeal. Walter Mondale addressed the concept of round tables in his acceptance speech at the 1984 Democratic National Convention. He pointed out that leadership in America has come from the grassroots since colonial times, and that it was in the presbyteries and meeting houses of pre-revolutionary America that our democracy was born. Even more basic than the "big issues" of the world are the responses we have to the issues that affect our daily lives. Local control educated colonial Americans to assume the responsibilities of free citizens. It can happen again today.

The importance of community involvement cannot be overstated. Projects such as KidsPlace in Seattle have involved not merely 6,700 children, but a wide range of community businesses, corporations, agencies and organizations working together with parents, teachers, and, of course, the kids.

But can local control really work? There is evidence that it does. John McKnight has described one project where community involvement led to a wide range of community activities that strengthened and supported that community, ultimately leading to the development of urban greenhouses to provide fresh food, new jobs, energy conservation, and recreational centers for senior citizens (McKnight, Personal Communication, 1977). In all his work McKnight emphasizes participation, recognizing that the community—non-professionals and consumers—can deal with issues we have most often professionalized; medical, legal, organizational, and community.

His example also serves to illustrate another important point—projects that improve health and well-being may have, seemingly, little to do with health. Yet a community garden in the Bronx, a cultural festival in Glasgow, a steam plant in Minneapolis, the threat of freeways in Toronto, a center for independent living for the disabled in Berkeley and waterfront development in Boston have all proved to be means to an end—providing a new focus for community action, and by strengthening the community, enhancing its health and the health of its members. In *Community Dreams* ("a collection of small-scale, local level ideas which can be set into motion in most communities by yourself and the people you know") Bill Berkowitz (1984) described literally hundreds of examples of community projects that focus on "altering the mindset with which we see our communities" and which imply that "we are most likely to find power and control, and gladness and joy, closest to where we live" (p. 235). His book is a potpourri of ideas for a healthy city.

More recently, McKnight and Kretzmann (1984) have suggested that we need "an organizing approach aimed at building community through the restoration of localized political economies." They suggest that we should try to enhance neighborhood as a locus for production and consumption through local community development corporations: the transfer of resources and authority to the neighborhood, perhaps through a return to a small portion of local taxes directly to neighborhood governments, and the re-establishment of business in the community.

Another possible strategy is an "anticipatory democracy" exercise. Such projects have been carried out successfully at the state level in a number of U.S. states (Marien, 1985, 110), as well as in a few cities (Marien, 1984, 129). In this process, a variety of plausible alternative future scenarios for the city are developed, widely disseminated and discussed in the community, then the community votes on which of the plausible scenarios is preferable. This can be a useful technique for establishing the city's values and goals as well as for securing community interest in the commitment to change.

There are apparently now more than 800,000 organizations concerned with self help in the U.S. It has long been central to our basic value system that all citizens should find a voice in governing themselves. This is not necessarily an easy or a peaceful process; the din may get overwhelming at times. Rising interest and rising voices attest a renewed citizen commitment to govern themselves. The hope, of course, is that people from all walks of life can reassert their power. People must come together—in round tables or other such groups—to ask questions about the significant issues that each community faces, then take actions to regain the "power to command the events that affect their lives."

We should also create nonpolarizing community-wide responses. The KidsPlace program of Seattle is an excellent example of such action. A broad, diverse group of citizens has come together to deal with a major problem of the city. They are unified in the ultimate goal, that of reversing an alarming population trend in their city, and they are dealing with this problem in diverse ways on many levels according to their particular talents.

Seattle, until recently, has had a reputation as a family town—a good place to raise kids. However, Seattle residents were dismayed to discover that at the very time the city was being proclaimed for its livability a great outmigration of families with children was taking place. In the decade between 1970 and 1980, while the overall population of the city declined 7 percent, the number of residents aged 18 and under declined a surprising 36 percent.

As Bruce Chapman of the White House Committee on Policy and Evaluation has said, "The city must have a living memory. You cannot import your whole population in each generation. If the public policy does not affirm the importance of families, then the city very possibly does not have a future." Robert Aldrich, University of Washington Medical School pediatrician, carried this a step further by pointing out that, "If you have a city that's not a place where children like to live, it eventually becomes a place where adults will not like to live."

To reverse the exodus of children, the mayor believes that not only is it important to change people's perceptions of Seattle as a place for young, affluent childless professionals, but the city must assess itself and make some appropriate changes, not only in services for children, but in giving them entré to other existing resources.

The project, KidsPlace, so named by the children of Seattle, was initiated to turn this population trend around. Through surveys, publicity and public participation, this project hopes to remind families who already live in the city of its advantages and it hopes to attract newcomers who now assume that children belong only in suburbia.

The first step, a simple word-association survey of what 60,000 of the city's school children think, was completed in June 1985. They were asked to identify places in Seattle brought to mind by words such as "helpful," "wet," "dangerous" and "fun." They were also asked what their favorite place in the city is, their favorite place to go with their parents, and what they would do to make Seattle a better place for kids if they were mayor.

Based on the results of the surveys, a review committee is in the process of selecting 20 projects that could be accomplished for about $1,000 each. For example, new benches could be installed at the aquarium that would be high enough for children to see into the tank that holds the sea otters. Certain community groups and businesses will fund these projects. The Junior League, for example, will pay for three such projects.

Most interesting is the broad spectrum of input into this project—in addition to that of the children themselves. It is being sponsored by the YMCA, the Junior League, and a private foundation that has contributed about $20,000 to start up the project. Private enterprise and government work side by side on this project. The regional office of the Department of Human Services of the U.S. Department of Health and Human Services, the City of Seattle and a private advertising firm will contribute services and funding. At least 20 community and academic groups will conduct studies examining issues such as child care, homeless youth and television violence. The effects of KidsPlace could be far-reaching.

Another strategy to create healthy cities is to recognize the new management styles. Corporate management styles that are proving successful today may have applications in our cities. Among the more interesting trends in corporate management in the U.S. today is that of participatory management and of employee ownership.

Another interesting management phenomenon is the "new populism" in America's business. Politically this trend has "radicalized" the middle class as individuals have looked for ways to resist external control by large government and institutions. Again, we see the effort, "to exert control over their own lives," an American ideal that goes back to the seventeenth century. This has had political implications (to cut down on Big Government) and, in corporate decision-making, it has created a demand for greater participation on the part of employee and public interest groups. Companies are now realizing that activist groups are no longer made up of housewives and radical revolutionaries *on the outside,* but of top executives and managers. They see that there are strong consumer and public interest groups *within* the corporate community, such as BENS, an anti-nuclear business group. Both of these trends can be observed in the operation of our cities today and how we deal with them can be important.

Another strategy is to become aware of and responsive to alternative education goals to produce "people who get things done." This involves working on the city's *soft* infrastructure. The research of behavioral scientists and educators in recent years indicates that the ways people have been taught in the past—to pass tests and show success in school—may not be the best way to teach people to think. Again, we turn to a corporate management model.

Recent research by Dr. Siegfried Strufert, a behavioral scientist at the Pennsylvania State University College of Medicine, suggests that most successful corporate leaders think in a way that he characterizes as "cognitively complex," his way of describing decision-making that does not depend on I.Q. This involves the capacity to acquire ample information for making decisions without being overwhelmed, and the ability to grasp relationships between rapidly changing events.

This view was substantiated earlier by Richard Boyatzis in his book, *The Competent Manager,* in which he identified 19 competencies in a study of more than 2,000 managers. Among these were being able to get different groups to collaborate well, being able to spot hidden patterns in an array of facts, and a sense of spontaneity in expressing themselves.

The ways these researchers describe thinking and decision-making is particularly applicable to the skills we have been talking about here in getting the parts of the city to work together.

Dr. Boyatzis describes a motive he calls "socialized power" as resulting in a "competency in which the person uses forms of influence to build alliances, networks, coalitions of teams.

With people trained in such thinking styles working in leadership roles in our cities the health of the cities could be affected positively.

The Goal: A Context for Success. Now, if in our efforts to make our city more healthy we have responded to the symptoms or dealt with the underlying issues, or both, we have set certain forces into motion. With sensitive, responsive, imaginative leadership we will have selected and implemented appropriate actions or programs that have created a context for success.

However this leadership must function *both* from the "top down" and the "bottom up." As in the health organism, the health of the parts as well as the vigor of the connections are essential to make the organism work at its highest level of competency. The context for success can only be created when the people of the city realize that if the context works for them they can solve their problems. It is then that the people of the city, working together in a spirit of reciprocal maintenance, can deal with the complex and multidimensional underlying issues of health to create their healthy city.

In Summary

For us, a healthy city is one that is engaged in a process of creating, expanding and improving those physical and social environments and community resources which enable people to mutually support each other in performing all the functions of life and developing to their maximum potential. A healthy city would have a clean, safe, high quality physical environment and would operate within its ecosystem in a manner that ensured the stability and sustainability of that ecosystem. The basic human needs of the city's people (food, water, shelter, income, safety, work) would be met. The community would be strong, mutually supportive and non-exploitative, participating actively in community governance. Individuals would have access to a wide variety of experiences and resources with the possibility of multiple contacts and interactions with other people. The city would have a vital, diverse economy, and its people would have a strong sense of connectedness with their biological and cultural heritage, with other groups and with individuals within the city. The city's form would be compatible with and support all of these circumstances, and there would be an optimum level of public health and appropriate sick care services accessible to all.

Such a city, were it to exist, would, we believe, have a high health status. But far more than that, it would be a healthy city in every sense of that term, a condition that must surely be the goal of all cities.

VII.

Conclusion: The Future Is Not What It Used To Be

In an earlier chapter, I explained that I chose health as a theme and focus for this study because health—somewhat like the idea of life itself—arouses little ideological ire in the politically rigid world of the late twentieth century. Health is a useful entry-point that arouses only minimal partisanship. It is important to stress again, however, that health was a choice of focus but it is not the *subject* of this work. There is a Buddhist saying that there are many paths up the mountain, but that once you start up a path it makes sense to stay on that path, because it is wasteful to climb down and start over. The peak is the same, no matter whether you start on the north or the south face. Health is one such path, and I have chosen it as apt for these times. But we could have chosen any number of others—economic development, education, housing, community organization, infra-structure, or a number of other themes. All roads lead to certain central issues— not to Rome, not to power and domination and the imposition of one culture on another—but all roads do lead to the center in a broader sense.

No matter what issues one starts with, whether it is water in Nepal or pollution in California, one finds that in dealing with the full implications of the issue, the map broadens to embrace all there is. One cannot, for example, impose family planning or compulsory education on the people of Nepal, because they need their children to continue to do what they are doing, which is to provide a precious and irreplaceable source of energy for the culture. The children carry water to the villages. The villages cannot survive without their energy. Upset this delicate balance, and the whole economic structure collapses. Schools, then, are intricately connected with the economy, the religion, and family values. Is the issue health? Not exactly, although it is a very complex planning issue. The women of Nepal will be released from constant child-bearing and the children of Nepal will be able to attend schools when resources can be found to transport water other than on the backs and heads of the young.

It would be simple, although somewhat odd, to say that by building pipes up the mountains one can get the children into school and the women out of childbed, but it is not even as simple as that. Nepal is desperately poor; it lacks the resources to build the pipes, and India has vetoed international loans that would help Nepal develop local energy industries that would lift it out of its desperate status. India is afraid that if it becomes dependent upon Nepalese energy, that it would be vulnerable to blackmail if the Chinese should invade Nepal. Now the secret to the education of the Nepalese children lies in Peking, and by extension, in Washington as well, and will take place when there is a relaxation of paranoia between the superpowers. In short, we are trying to plan in a pathological world; when one major part of the complex web is as troubled as international relations are today, the effects are felt right down to the village level. On the positive side, however, because of the inter-connections of seemingly disparate spheres, one can intervene anywhere in the system with effects that ripple way beyond the intended consequences. Working for a nuclear freeze may indirectly help the children of Nepal get the water jugs off their backs.

But this is not a hierarchical world, where effects trickle down from Moscow, Washington, or Peking. The flow of energy goes both ways. Intervening on the village level in Nepal, or perhaps more effectively to soothe relationships between the Nepalese and the Indians so that the development loans can go through, may have its effects on all levels around, from the local village children right to the centers of world power. When dealing with centers of world power, as in the Nepalese case, they are not included so that they will intervene in some big-brother fashion to solve the issues of the lesser peoples of the earth. The point is that when Washington and Peking and Moscow solve their *own* problems, then the Indians and Nepalese will be free to solve theirs.

Nepal is a worst-case example, a country with almost no infrastructure, a classical "Fourth World" country caught between hostile great powers and lacking even in the natural resources with which other relatively powerless minor nations obtain some bargaining clout. Even in Nepal, however, there are limited programs that work to help local people develop competence—and the development of local competence has been a key theme of this book. Reforestation is one such program, and other programs dealing with such basics as water and food and child health are under way. One cannot predict the results at this point except to suggest that to some extent, however limited, they will affect us all.

Because of the connecting webs of international markets, international communications, and the unprecedented numbers of people who move now between cultures and from country to town, there are truly no longer any isolated planning issues or untouched cultures. We have all been brought into the same arena. The boundaries between fields and problems are breaking down, and all issues must be seen in a complex, multi-dimensional fashion. There is no single way to view a given problem—and this means that any intervention, no matter how misguided, is going to have some consequences. We have, in short, a redundancy of choice, more in California today than in Nepal, more in rich and educated cultures than in poor cultures with undeveloped infrastructures. *All interventions have impact.*

But although we are all in the same arena, we still live according to our own realities, planners no less than ghetto blacks or Nepalese Buddhists. The error of Western planning in the past has been to impose its technical model willy-nilly on disparate situations for which it is unsuited, to try to push everyone into a single system. The task for the present is a new one—to educate people so that they can choose the particular reality best suited to deal with a particular problem. Those concerned with change have to envision multiple maps, nested, interlocking, interconnecting, multi-level systems. Planners need flexibility and fast footwork to intervene effectively.

The change entrepreneurs need also to remain unattached to the particular strategy they have chosen at any one time. Although they need to keep fundamental human values in mind, they need to intervene where it is possible to intervene, even if this does not fit their model of how the world *should* be. In many religious traditions, people train for years in the most rigorous ways simply to be able to see things *as they are,* without illusion or distortion. So the injunction for planners to work with the system as it is rather than how they wish it were is not a simple one. Abandoning the safe, specialized ground of

Western data-collection for this new world of multiple realities and co-dependence can be a disorienting experience.

In working this way, beyond one's own fear, one has to deal with the fear and resistance of co-workers and of clients. The rule here is not to challenge conceptual systems directly, but to begin with people where they are. If cost-containment is on people's minds, as in California, talk cost-containment. You can use their reality, their conceptual frame, and their obsessions, and still make major changes.

The point for planners is not to have single products to sell but to be able to deal flexibly with a world of organized complexity and varying degrees of rigidity. If a change entrepreneur finds institutional rigidity and resistance in one place, he can bloody his head butting it against the stone walls, or he can walk around that wall and work someplace else. Because the system we are dealing with is world-wide, we can literally start anywhere—as long as we are not attached to a particular vision of how things should be.

A classical example of walking around a wall of resistance is the work in medical education done by John Rhode, formerly of the Rockefeller Foundation. Rhode, finding medical reform difficult in the United States, knew that he had a redundancy of choices; he kept moving, seeking other paths up the mountain, and he performed his work in Indonesia in a masterful end run and brought the lesson back to the United States.

Briefly, Rhode had worked in the United States—specifically medical education—a discipline that paid little more than lip service to prevention, community medicine, and other forms of primary care. Medical education in the West since 1910 or so has moved, as everyone knows, more and more in the direction of high technology, scientific, specialized medicine, with results that do not justify the enormous expenditures for medical education and medical care. Medicine in the West in the last generation or two, in spite of its soaring costs, has done little to improve the health of the populace. Community medicine would solve many of the simple problems of maternal and child health, family pathology, alcoholism, addiction, and other social-medical problems that continue to take their toll in the inner cities, rural slums and suburbs of the United States. Rhode, however, working out of the Rockefeller Foundation, and others were unable to get medical schools in America to look seriously at revising their curricula in the direction of more community medicine.

Instead of giving up, or moving into an elder-statesman role of social criticism, from which lofty perch he could write clever and bitter articles for the *Atlantic* and the Sunday *Times* about the impossibility of reforming the corrupt and rigid American medical system, Rhode and his colleagues moved out of the American system. Rhode went to Indonesia where he worked with local officials to establish a community-medicine oriented medical school designed to meet the particular needs of the Indonesian populace. A recent visit there shows that this program is working, although limited in impact, and that it meets the health needs of the Indonesians aptly.

The next step for Rhode and the Foundation is to use the success of community medicine in Indonesia to persuade the American medical schools to institute similar programs in this country. There is a good chance to succeed at this, whereas if he had stayed here and had to hammer away at the medical schools for the years that he was building his program in Indonesia, little would have been accomplished here or there.

The Rhode story brings us back to the question of values, to what, in the broadest sense, the planner is trying to accomplish. If we are not selling a program, a model, a well-defined vision of our goals, and if it does not matter where we start, then what are we up to? Is it not dangerously vague to assert that the planner can begin anywhere and intervene at any level without even having a fixed model of his desired outcome? Are we not inviting chaos? Are we more than opportunists?

We are trying to plan in a world with multiple interlocking value systems, and we are trying to devise planning approaches that avoid the old mistakes of Western planners, which were to carry their own values of technical competence and material success into cultures for which they were ill-suited and maladaptive. In the past, Western planners designed systems that fit a single value system—a Western value system—and because of the dominant Western myth that the social sciences were "objective"—and could access reality, many planners imposed culture-bound, Western values on cultures for which they were alien. They had a single model of planning and of development and of the way they thought things should be, and they brought these "objective" truths to other cultures with an almost missionary zeal.

In the world as we are beginning to understand it, however, people have to learn to communicate on multiple levels of value systems. There is not a single, world-wide game with a single set of rules. No universal model suffices. Planners must first, then, become aware of, and to some extent comfortable with, this complexity of system, and they must learn, not only the different value-game systems, but more importantly, become meta-players. They must learn the processes by which people learn how to play according to one set of rules or another. They must learn how to learn—and teach others to do so.

The planning challenge, then, is to design a gameboard where multiple sets of values can be negotiated on a single field. The first thing the planner has to recognize is that he is not outside the system. There is no value-free planning. The planner carries his own values into this process. So the good planner, like the good therapist, must learn what he brings to the system and how he changes it, before beginning to deal with clients. The first map one has to chart is the map of one's own mind. There are no objective observers outside the field.

This means that the planner's loyalty goes outside of particular organizations and specific goals. Most people function, however, with smaller maps, one organizational set of rules. They work to preserve the organization—the medical school, the hospital, the agency—rather than to achieve the goals for which the organization was originally established. The good planner is, ultimately, a poor organization man. But he cannot begin that way. As he develops his competence in the fields that he will use, he has to build up credit in his own bailiwick. He cannot *begin* by flying around in the cracks between systems. But even when he is working within a single gameboard, on a single set of rules, the good planner is developing his broader map-making skills and working to build connections with the other games in town. One must work for acceptance and respectability in one's own field before trying to transcend it. With the dizzying pace of change in the world of the eighties, it is impossible to be effective if one gets stuck defending a little piece of turf.

The planner is ultimately working on *trust;* he trusts that those with whom he is working know what they need in terms of their own values and culture, and he trusts that he can help stimulate them to develop competence to achieve it. Competence to shape one's own life is health—and it is freedom. These are the ultimate values behind our vision of planning. In the institutional ferment and chaos of the current world, the planner can hope to stimulate others to create new forms that will meet their needs.

The change entrepreneur, then, is working in a non-hierarchical mode. He is not imposing the values of his "superior" culture and technology on a benighted and ignorant people. He has learned to live in a world that is relative, complex, multivalent, uncertain, changing, and in many respects unknown. Not for him are the simplifications of a bi-polar world, God and the devil, Washington and Moscow. We repeat, however, that this value-free, non-control model for the planner is easier to describe than to implement. To be human is to be located, to have positions, ideas, values, and some wish to control the world around one. One's goals as an effective planner are therefore twofold: to be aware, as much as possible, what one's own distorting lenses may be, what one's own personal and cultural values are; and secondly, to have access to multiple models of reality, so that one is not trying to fit everyone into a single mode.

In addition, if one is stimulating others to create their own infrastructures in terms of their own beliefs and values, one is also teaching others what one is learning for oneself. One does not just learn how to use various skills, dig latrines, clean the village well, or build a community center. One is learning as well *how to learn*, how to change, and how to be together in new ways. One is creating new institutional forms that are flexible, adaptable, and non-hierarchical. The change entrepreneur is truly a facilitator. This approach can most dramatically be seen in the Sarvodaya self-help movement that is transforming rural Sri Lanka, as described in an earlier chapter. Ariyaratne, the founder of the movement, has said repeatedly, "A country cannot develop unless one has faith in the intelligence of the people."

Freedom, schizophrenia, and enlightenment take place in the cracks between categories, in the undefined spaces between thoughts, where our organizing, cognitive categories are momentarily in suspension. This is why crisis offers danger and opportunity simultaneously. At moments of crisis all potential shows again, and all organization, which has been a narrowing and an exclusion, is broken up for a time. The cultural repetition compulsion is suspended for a time, and there is the opportunity to do the new. A culture is, like a self or a personality, a pressure and a momentum to repeat old patterns. Crisis, such as the crisis of decolonialization in Sri Lanka, can stimulate change in the direction of creative growth, or it can lead to chaos, anarchy, and tyranny.

In the perfect plan, no one makes a mistake. The universe is completely under control; nothing unforeseen or unexpected happens. But in the true social learning situation that is real life, mistakes are acceptable. There can be no action without risk, and no real change without error. This is why we stress the process, rather than the outcome. Health, too, is not an outcome or a product but a process. Health is the movement toward health. Change is the striving toward change.

In every crisis there is opportunity, if one is willing to risk, if one has the imagination to see the positive potential, and if one can break out of the repetition compulsion that is culture. The more open the system, the more likelihood there will be that such risks will be taken. No organization should change too quickly, however, or it is in danger of falling into chaos. It is essential to maintain a balance between change and stability. Because change involves risk and the certainty that there will be mistakes, too intense a period of change can overwhelm and paralyze a system or an individual. The learning from mistakes that *is* social learning cannot take place too quickly, or the system may become unable to function, the individuals in it may lose confidence, and a kind of institutional depression may set in. "This is not working," the floating leadership may decide, and anarchy or the resumption of strict hierarchy (or new forms of tyranny) may ensue.

In the process of change, a floating leadership—as in the Sarvodaya movement—is most effective and most receptive to social learning, for two reasons. First of all, there are more individuals investing their creativity into the system, so that more human energy is mobilized, and so that passivity and a sense of helplessness are diminished. Secondly, the process of social learning is automatically diffused throughout the system. The entire system becomes more flexible, adaptable, and responsible—as in responsive, capable of *response*. The energy of the oppressed is liberated into the system. It takes a lot of energy, on the individual level, to maintain a repression. Neurotics get tired. So, too, on the social level, the repression of large groups of people, their exclusion from real participation in the process of change, in social learning, squanders human energy. Release this energy— slowly, carefully, perhaps in the context of spiritual values and service as in Sri Lanka—and a thousand flowers may bloom. This is a society that is *learning to change;* the *process* of continual responsiveness is the very goal we seek. There will be no point where it all stops and the perfect society ensues.

Change does not stop, much as the controllers would like it to. This is why fixed models, rigid conceptual frameworks, whether derived from Marx or Locke, ultimately do not work. All living things bend and sway and flow. It is death—homeostasis—when the process stops, that is rigid and stiff. The mind is attracted by death; it wants to pause and fix and make certain. It wants to control, to know, to stop the process so that it can *see* it. But the stopping is murder; it kills and stills and stiffens. Life, growing around conceptual rigidity, becomes warped and deformed, like roots around rocks. It takes a lot of energy to push people down; it takes a lot of energy to sell them your model of the universe, when all their experience convinces them that it does not match their experience. Human beings can be forced, for a time, to go along with a system they do not trust, they can be terrorized into it, but the waste is appalling. It is a death trip.

The changer then, the facilitator, the "helper," ultimately helps himself. The only real evaluation to take place is self-evaluation. The idea is to trust that each living thing knows best what it needs—on some level, we all know, and can often say, if just symbolically, what we need in order to grow and be healthy. Even a schizophrenic adolescent who may be unable to speak coherently can sometimes draw, mime, or sing a diagnosis and a cure. But what then is the role of the helper? What does the changer do? In some sense, he or she *has* to help in order to live, and it is being done ultimately for oneself. Like the recovered alcoholic whose sobriety depends on 12th-step work, that is, on the continuous effort to help free others from alcoholism, the work is essentially done, not for the new AA members, but for oneself. He is helping himself. He has to do it.

What this also means is that programs may not need to be monitored in the way that traditional planning agencies have done them. If rules or standards are not imposed from above, it may be most desirable merely to make change possible—give out some money, supply some equipment—and let the grantees proceed relatively unsupervised. This involves *trust,* the genuine belief that people know what they need to do and will do it with energy and without corruption. In some cases, the money may be misused, but one wonders if possible waste or corruption is any more expensive than the enormous amount that needs to be expended to maintain a monitoring, overseeing, bureaucracy. And the *process* of trust may be far better for the recipients of this aid, for it empowers them. They are out of their client, child-like position. They do not have to play submission games with the overseeing bureaucracy. They have become grownups. Self-image improves— as in the Sarvodaya movement. Trust begets confidence.

It has taken the Americans generations of aid programs to learn that the world cannot solve its problems by using the American model, the American imperative to *play our game or else.* Our clients world-wide literally *cannot* play our game in many cases, and it has taken a long time for us to look back at ourselves, to evaluate our own game itself and see what is omitted, to see why it does not work. The learning flow has not reversed itself completely yet—the enormous momentum of our cognitive and institutional thrust is such that social learning is difficult for us. But we are at the point of self-assessment, the point of self-evaluation where everyone who wants to change things should start. As we look at the shortcomings in our own models of change, derived as they have been from a Western scientific model that was based on a sharp separation (to many it seems automatic, the Way Things Are) between subject and object, between self and world, a system that was based on the myth of the objective observer, one of the most powerful religious beliefs ever invented, we begin to see that the world we have been trying to teach and change may have something to teach us. For an obsessive culture that does not like to be wrong, this may feel like humiliation—and there have been American actions in the last generation that have expressed this sense of humiliation, defeat, and rage.

What does the Third World see when it looks back at us, when it finds its voice again? Senegal's Leopold Senghor has noted that the Western philosophic and scientific tradition attempted to know objects by separating them from the observer, but that even in the West, recent developments have cast grave doubts on such a method. The traditional African method of reasoning, by contrast, is "intuitive by participation;" it holds that to know something one must experience it.

Aime Cesaire, a West Indian poet, has expressed this rejection of Western values and rediscovery of the ancient, non-Western alternative in the following lines:

Listen to the white world
how it resents its great efforts
how their protest is broken under the rigid stars
How their steel blue is paralyzed in the mystery of the flesh.
Listen how their defeats sound from their victories.
Listen to the lamentable stumbling in the great alibis.
Mercy! Mercy for our omniscient naive conquerors.
Hurrah for those who never invented anything.
Hurrah for those who never explored anything.
Hurrah for those who never conquered anything.
Hurrah for joy.
Hurrah for love.
Hurrah for the pain of incarnate tears.

Cesaire's reaction, however, may discard too much. It seems to me that the ideal would be a balance, a melding of the technological skills of the West, incorporated and subdued within the ancient, human value structures still expressed in the Eastern and Southern cultures, in the Buddhism of the Sarvodaya movement, in the African values of learning by intuitive participation, in the Hinduism of Bali. The world is still basically oppressive—the North oppresses the South and reactions like Cesaire's are understandable responses to this oppression. But he looks back to a world that cannot be recovered, beautiful as it may have been. He, too, expresses a dichotomy, a separation of self and other, oppressor and oppressed, West and East, North and South, that is ultimately unhealthy. He, too, is seduced by the past. The two visions need each other. The Sarvodaya movement builds roads, sewers, schools, and other technological monuments *within the context* of Buddhist values of intuitive participation, community, selflessness, and compassion. It is this blending that the world needs. This takes the best of East and West and creates something new. Ariyaratne is not stalled in Cesaire's hurrahs for stasis.

The changer, like Donald Schon's "reflective practitioner," does not operate in the world by applying knowledge. Whether as a therapist or as a politician, the emphasis is not mainly on content but on process. Schon establishes this as the first principle in his recent study of how professionals think in action. We would add to his analysis that the process in which the changer becomes involved is complex and multileveled. The practitioner confronts the individual or organizational client on an enormous number of levels, from the individual body system and intrapsychic systems of the clients, to the interplay between them, to the client in a number of family systems and subsystems, to the developmental history of the clients, the family or origin, and finally to the clients' many systems as they interact with each other and with the larger world. So, although it is true that the professional, the practitioner, the changer, focuses on process, process itself is enormously complex. A choice has to be made about what level intervention should start at, although intervention at any level, because of the interconnectedness of the many systems, will reverberate throughout them all. The practitioner needs to seek the "key leverage points" described in an earlier chapter and intervene there.

Schon does argue that the practitioner uses a multiplicity of theories, and that he is always ready to adapt a theory to a given situation. He is, in short, constantly improvising. The basis of his thinking, Schon goes on to say, is phenomenological. He is not an applied social scientist, not really a scientist at all, but both scientist and artist and perhaps something more. Schon discusses the necessity for the practitioner to have empathy with the situation, a Western way to talk about the "intuition by participation" of which many Eastern and Southern cultures speak. His analysis could be extended here to the Buddhists' idea of compassion, the energy of the great teacher, and that all Buddhist teachings stress that this compassion begins with the self. All acts of compassion or empathy reverberate positively throughout the universe, even of acts of compassion to the self, self love. Compassion and knowledge of the self go together, and the process, the internal process, of the practitioner himself is as essential as the empathy of which Schon speaks. This self-knowledge is absolutely essential, for the change entrepreneur cannot know a situation until he knows what he brings to it and how he changes it by his presence. Looking outward for knowledge brings us back to the self and its knowing structures, just as the search within takes us, if pursued with its full vigor, to the universe.

This begins to sound as if the change entrepreneur is artist, scientist, and perhaps shaman, although it is doubtful that many Western professionals would welcome that designation. In any event, empathy, intuitive participation, something more than the application of technique, is essential in what he is doing. The changer also works in a situation of not knowing a good deal of the time. He needs to be able to *act* in a situation of ambiguity and uncertainty. He needs to be able to risk working with multiple paradigms.

Schon's principles apply to the individual practitioner, but he does not talk about the ways in which teams and networks operate together to create change, as in Arie's Sri Lanka movement. In such team efforts, leadership is floating, and skills are built up through the process of social learning throughout the team. The goal is to disperse leadership skills and basic competence throughout the system, in short, to deprofessionalize it without, however, in any way demeaning professionalism. Professional skills are essential to social learning and social change; they become obstacles to change when the professional's main goal becomes the effort to protect his professional territory and cognitive executiveness. But the skills themselves, the competence, if allowed to diffuse throughout the system, are welcome.

If the sewer builders in Sri Lanka were to start a guild in which only they were licensed to build and repair sewers and that towns who wanted a sewer or a drainage repair had to call a licensed sewer-contractor, wait for him to arrive, and pay him the fee he had set, this would be, in parody form, the situation of professionalism in the West today. Its entire spirit would go against all that Ariyaratne is trying to build in Sri Lanka, which is the diffusion of competence, confidence, leadership, and skill throughout the system, throughout the entire society. It is at this point, about opening up the change situation to all members of a group and not to locate change in the person of the professional practitioner, that we go beyond Schon's excellent and provocative principles.

The principle, then, is to *think globally, act locally.* And in order to act locally, one must know and use the local map. Infrastructures and leverage points will vary from place to place. The Sarvodaya movement, for example, has an invisible but powerful infrastructure available to it that mobilizes human energies in the villages, and that is the shared values of Buddhism. These provide a framework for selfless action, and the Buddhist world view offers villagers a sense of connection to the entire universe as they labor on their village projects. The people of Sri Lanka can use this invisible and powerful infrastructure as they build the other, material infrastructures that they lack.

In the West, by contrast, the material infrastructures are in place and functioning with redundant efficiency whereas the spiritual and ideological structures are fragmented, incomplete, and too often counsels of despair and cynicism. The question here is how to reincorporate spiritual values, human values, generosity, selflessness, and community into a culture that has lost them, and more than that, does not think they are possible. There is no value-free planning; but what are our values? It is at this point that the West can look at its conquered peoples, at the post-colonial world, for these cultures, whether they be Buddhists in Sri Lanka or shamans in the American Southwest, speak of wholeness, divinity, and non-separation. Their maps of the world are more complex and complete than are Western maps, whether these be maps of disease and illness or descriptions of the mind. They can offer us values, connection, and healing. They are not afraid to speak of love. They have not suffered the fragmentation and specialization that have torn our Western world-view into disconnected bits. They do not attempt to reduce all phenomena to one kind of explanation, such as economic or biological.

Can we take human values and use our infrastructures to implement them? To do so will mean abandoning old fixed notions of how things are. For many liberals, for example, Safeway stores are the villain, representing all that is big and polluting and dehumanizing in Western corporate capitalism. But what if one shifts one's picture a little bit, jiggles the map, and sees Safeway as a potential *resource* to accomplish certain human goals. There is hunger in America today while food rots in fields and warehouses and the back rooms of supermarkets. The problem is *distribution,* getting the excess food to those who need it.

The people who work in the poverty field have tried to *build* distribution systems, an expensive and difficult process, especially for people without experience in business. Meanwhile, the impressive Safeway distribution system sits there, efficiently going about its business and getting food to the affluent. What would happen if this system could be *rented* to get food to the poor as well? It would be cheaper than building an entire parallel distribution system, it would do the job, and it would bring together old enemies to work for human values. Safeway, however, should not have to be convinced to be generous; they can work with their old values, profit, self interest, and efficiency. But the job could be done, once the crucial shift takes place, the map-making, conceptual shift that sees Safeway not as the Enemy of the Proletariat but simply as a resource, a neutral field. Will Safeway corporate values shift because of its participation in a food distribution system to the poor? No one can say, but it seems possible. Will the perception of Safeway held by those who benefit from the food distribution system change? Again, it seems possible. In any event, more of the available structures in the Western community have been utilized for human purposes.

If politics is the art of asking people what they want rather than imposing it from the top down, it is true that the degree of participation will vary according to community and place. In Sri Lanka, participatory politics, decentralization, and local decision-making seem to be working effectively. In Thailand, on the other hand, the model for change seems to be at the present time much more paternal, top-down, and hierarchical. The King of Thailand sees himself as the soul of his nation whose goal is to meet the needs of his population. In order to do this, he travels 210 days per year, visiting the villages to determine their needs and respond to them. Given the situation in Thailand, this almost medieval model of the beneficent ruler seems to work most effectively for change. The point is to start where people *are* and work from that.

As an example, the head of the Thai population program, Michai, has been dealing with problems of over-population. Here the process is not to ask people what they want, for what they want is more children, because children make up such a valuable energy source. So Michai's work is to impose a change on the people, to introduce contraception to a resistant population. He does so in a number of clever ways including making condoms *popular* by holding condom parties, having condom trinkets, and other advertising methods. He also uses a gentle form of bribery: if you use condoms, the government will loan you money for a rice bank, loan you a buffalo for the village, offer other economic incentives. In order to introduce new and improved breeds of rice to the resistant peasant economy, Michai offers it as a reward for using condoms. In other words, he slowly invades and transforms all village systems in the name of condoms. In the process, he is also building local community and competence. In order to have a rice bank, the villagers must hold a meeting; there are also condom parties. These meetings and gatherings bring the villagers together in a new way, and begin to build community in much the way the Sarvodaya work days do in Sri Lanka.

What Michai is doing is dealing with immediate issues while he also begins a process that will create a new political infrastructure in Thailand. As the people meet together to discuss the rice bank or the water tanks under the Temple, they are learning *how to meet*. A process of social learning has begun to take place. Most politicians shoot from the hip; they come in with quick fixes and then leave. Michai is solving immediate problems while he also opens up the process of social learning that will transform the society in the long run.

A similar process began to take place in California. What is described sadly was vetoed by the Governor. The lessons are nevertheless still valid. The state, like all jurisdictions in the 1980s, has suffered severe cutbacks in its mental health budget, so that agencies are deploring the shortage and fighting over scraps of the skimpy pie. The Select Committee on Mental Health, faced with this program, orchestrated a social learning process that makes an end run around the money shortages and does not confront them directly. This end run is in accordance with the fundamental unstated assumption of this book: *If you run into a brick wall, do not bang your head on it unless you like having a bloody head.* But, in fact, to argue about money within the existing program would have gotten the Assembly Committee no place. It would involve no cognitive restructuring, no fresh mapmaking, no open space for creativity to emerge. It would confine one to a hopeless repetition of the old, exhausted game.

Instead, the Committee, like a crab against a rock, moved sideways. The Select Committee on Mental Health was, in fact, a new committee, set up especially this year without a constraining past to cope with the mental health crisis in California. Instead of confronting budget shortages, the Committee has set out to create a new mental health map for the state. They did this by inquiring of every mental health professional in the state about diagnosis and treatment. What is the best current knowledge in the field about schizophrenia, depression, and other classical diagnostic categories?

This inquiry, however, was only the first step. It was designed to stimulate activity at the local level, so that those on the line begin to think about what they are doing, about what mental health and illness is. It was designed to create ferment, to break routines, to perhaps foster irritation ("What do they want *this* for?"), to shake things up, and to stimulate creativity. The original questionnaire was designed within the classical categories of psychiatry, the DSM III categories that rule orthodoxy in the field. This in itself should stimulate those who are exploring creative alternatives such as family therapy or Gestalt to speak out, and a dialogue begins.

On the second round of questions mental health professionals in the hospitals, clinics, and private practice will be asked by Sacramento about where disturbed children can first be identified. Is it in first grade? Second grade? Where is schizophrenia first evident? Developmental disorders? Learning disabilities? What patterns of illness and treatment do they see? Is it true that the rich get therapy and the poor get drugs? What is their current assessment of race and mental illness, ethnicity, gender, occupation, diet, and stress? At each stage of this questionnaire process, the professionals in the field are enticed to answer by the promise that they will receive the results of the studies, tabulated, and summarized. These summaries will also serve to orchestrate the social learning process. Given these results, the study summaries will say, can we perhaps construct a new model for mental health? What is the true map for mental health? Whose business is it? What is the true constituency? You professionals are now faced with budget shortages so severe that you can barely do your job, but is mental health your job alone? Who else can help you? If, as your responses show, mental health is a matter of the entire environment, if it is affected by traffic, the home, the school, the workplace, the supermarket, and the popular press, it seems that mental health is everyone's business. Who can help you do your job? Can we ask everyone to help? Can we ask business, labor, the teaching profession, and the press?

The goal of this innocent questionnaire is to change mental health in the entire state, to make it holistic and environmental, to make it contextual and to break it away from the medical model that has isolated it in a professional bailiwick where it is starving for funds. The goal is to make a new map, to broaden the constituency, and to open up the subject so that new creativity can emerge. In the process, those professionals who are defending an institution, a set of beliefs, a turf, are going to feel uncomfortable and threatened, but they, too, can eventually be brought into the statewide social learning process or they can be bypassed if necessary. One of the advantages of having the long view is that generations pass. Old Freudians retire. One can duck the boss and appeal to his frustrated subordinates. It is in some measure to these frustrated subordinates that much of this book has been addressed, to give them energy and hope and encourage them not to give up. There is a network of such people in institutions around the state, often working without knowledge of their peers elsewhere, entrepreneurial spirits who think contextually but feel isolated within the organizational structure within which they are embedded. Processes such as the Select Committee questionnaires can put such people in contact with each other, allow them room to breathe outside of the orthodoxies of the institution within which they are confined. All institutions embody the past; even the most flexible is yet a frozen structure, a barrier and dam, a wall or a set of walls. Water flows around walls, however, and it is such a flow that I wish to encourage here. The boss may never be convinced. He does not have to be. Translate what you are doing into his language, so that he can file it into his own cognitive structure, and *get on with it*. You do not need to break down the walls in order to move, nor do you have to convince people in direct confrontation, nor do you need to bloody your head and retire with a hopeless tension headache. It is possible to walk around the wall. The key is patience and persistence and faith.

The process of information gathering is, in fact, health. This process involves working on all levels at once, instead of selling out to a fragment. At the same time, while keeping the larger map in mind, the questionnaire starts out with mental health professionals where they are, with the diagnostic categories of DSM III. You can start anywhere, with any language, AS LONG AS YOU KEEP THE BIGGEST POSSIBLE MAP IN YOUR MIND. A second principle about the map, however, is that it is only a map. Even the biggest and most comprehensive one should not be mistaken for reality. Endless, stupid wars have been fought by those who had fallen in love with their maps and mistook them for reality. All maps should come with an Operation Destruct Button. All maps, like all institutions, are pieces of the past, fixed structures.

If the dream is an event, and the story exists for itself beyond whatever we may be able to make of it, what, then, has this book been about? I have addressed most of our intervention strategies not at how to *act* but rather, how to *see* in a way that our seeing does not impoverish reality. I have called for human intelligence to live with fresh stories, whether on the individual level or in the institutions that have grown and been created to express us. Stories touch us more deeply than plans do; they speak to more aspects of our beings. For this reason, they can create unease in those who want reality to be clear and structured and predictable. Stories *enchant* reality.

I have tried here to incorporate new ways of thinking on the far side of objectivity. The illusion of the objective social sciences was that the observer was safe; he (and the observer, the planner or scientist, was most likely to be a *he*) was removed from the risks and falls and movement he was observing. To observe was a way to be perfect, still, unchanging, and safe.

But there is no platform on which to stand that holds still and that is out of the flux. Observer and observed are equally part of the whole and equally vulnerable. I have said this in many ways as I have gone through the process of writing this book, and I have experienced my own vulnerability as I have traversed this time. My experiences and the way I have shared them with others, have changed the content of what I have written here. Conferences about the ideas in this book have been a somewhat unusual mixture of the personal and the theoretical as I and others have attempted to live and integrate in our own lives what I have written about here. Life is not linear, and we have been faced with abundant evidence in these past few years that it is certainly not to be controlled.

Often it seemed to me that events came to illustrate a point about multiple realities, to show the permeable boundaries between categories such as madness and sanity, or to show a direction when the writing became stalled. The process of making this book was on multiple levels of personal and family friendship and professional association that changed and deepened over time.

What has this book been about? I have said repeatedly what it is NOT—that it is not only about health, community therapy, or planning. The hope I have is that the book will provoke, stimulate, and irritate, that it will evoke response in perhaps unpredictable ways. I have been immersed in life, as children like to be in water, while I have worked on this manuscript, and this immersion has been brought to the surface in conversations whose meaning was not always clear to me and whose common theme emerged only in the course of them. The book unfolded; I myself could not predict its contents.

The theme, if there is one, has been change, both how to live with it in a healthy way and how to provoke it where necessary. There are enormous human tendencies toward stasis, towards the safety of stillness, the ultimate symbol of which is death. But although I began with the clear linear idea that the book should be about change, things happened in both my personal and professional life that introduced other possibly tangential themes.

Appendix I

Health and the Inner and Outer Sky

For many years I have thought about health and illness almost always in the context of the totality of existence. I believe that the idea of health in isolation from wholeness has little meaning. The very language we speak acknowledges the connection between health and the whole, although most of us have forgotten that the words health, healing, whole, and holy all come from the same root. In this discussion of health and sky, then, I do not separate health from *manus*—the hand of God—or from the wholeness of all that is. Health, of course, means more than the absence of illness; it has to do with the way we feel and interact with everything around us. As Rene Dubos has written, health is the ability to use all our senses, all aspects of mind, body, and soul.

When I contemplate the sky and its connection to health, it becomes increasingly clear to me, as I sort out my knowledge, beliefs, concepts, and memories, that this wholeness I refer to is indeed the totality of the universe. The sky is a symbol of universal vastness, openness, and nearly unimaginable meaning, and at the same time, it cannot be separated from myself, from my own health and the health of all who live. We carry the universe, both vast space and intricate form, within us, although we live—I have lived—for the most part alienated from any knowledge of this intimate link between body-minds and sky. On the straight shelves of the bookcases in my boxy house I have rectangular books that tell me of this connection between inner and outer space, books such as Timothy Ferris's *Galaxies* and Lennart Neillson's *Behold Man,* in which the images of outer space are almost indistinguishable from the inner physical spaces so beautifully portrayed in Neillson's photographs.

There is an ever-expanding literature that evokes such connections, not only between inner and outer space, but between disciplines conventionally thought of as distinct, even antithetical, between, for example, the discoveries of modern science and the visionary worlds reported by anthropologists, students of the myth, and spiritual teachers. Scientific theories in recent years have born an eerie resemblance to the dream world of speculation, ritual, religion and myth. If a modern physicist tells us that we can reach the farthest stars, not by building better spaceships, but rather by transforming our consciousness, it sounds as if a poet is speaking, or a shaman, or a master of the occult. When our physicists and astronomers explain that what we see depends on who is looking and how the looking is done, because the observer cannot be separated from the observed, these scientists seem to echo this haunting epigram of the Kalahari Pygmies, "There is a dream dreaming us."

And yet these connections cannot be proven, at least not with the normal proofs by which Western scientists establish theories. Our knowledge—if it is knowledge—seems to go beyond the world of scientific theory to vaster spaces, spaces that are inchoate, awe-inspiring, and yet somehow familiar. We all know these worlds or have glimpsed them as children, or during crises, or perhaps when on drugs, although we often hesitate to speak about them. These experiences are too personal, too idiosyncratic, and too unscientific to bear on our serious professional work—or so we tell ourselves.

Some years ago a group of people, including myself, was asked by the Outdoor Recreation Resources Review Commission whether the outdoor environment, the national parks and open space, were important for the mental health of individuals. We could only conclude in the affirmative, although we admitted that our data was subjective and experiential and would not pass muster by the usual scientific methodological criteria. How, indeed, would one *prove* such a relationship. And yet, if in some sense we and the sky are one, then health and the sky have many connections. We *know* this, if only from those very personal and idiosyncratic experiences that professionals tend to discount because they do not constitute "hard" evidence.

I would like to share two childhood experiences that changed my life profoundly, although until quite recently I did not recognize that these moments of joy, light, and birth bore any crucial connection to my professional work in health and mental health. But of course they do. They had to do with the sky, light, birth and health.

The first of these experiences happened in 1939 when I was 13 years old and on a midsummer overnight hike in the Massachusetts Berkshires. I awoke in the middle of the night to a spectacular jeweled sky. There were stars I had never seen before, and they all sparkled with an intimate brilliance that riveted me to them. I was captured by a state of awe for many hours and then slept. Waking in the morning after only a short sleep, I felt alive and vital, refreshed, full of energy, and with a sense of well-being that I can recapture even now.

On another adolescent outing in the summer of 1942, I left my bed at 5:30 a.m. and as the light came up, I walked along a trail through the morning mist. I stopped as spiders wove their webs on dewy branches. The trail meandered along the Sawkill River, a tiny stream in Dutchess County, New York. I passed the steamy falls, and crossed the water, which in the dawn light shone through summer leaves. Across the stream, I pushed through the underbrush, climbed a hill to the edge of the woods, and came to a golf course sandtrap, damp with dew and speckled with silver and gold. Furrowing this radiance were footprints of tiny creatures and at the end of each feathery trail, I found a miniature wood turtle. I picked one up and looked and returned him to his path. I traced the trails back and found a nest of small brownish-white eggs, some whole, some cracked, and one or two just cracking.

I sat enchanted, watching. The sun rose; the colors changed; the dew slowly melted away; and the newborn turtles emerged with the light. A state of awe surrounded me. All but my focused attention on the hatching disappeared. Time passed. I watched as the turtles one by one vanished in the nearby woods. I left, walking as if above ground, buoyant, vital, and filled with a vibrant sense of excitement.

I have had flashes of similar experiences as an adult; for example, walking along a Pacific beach at night, sensing waves, sand, rocks and sky and at one moment kicking a pine cone and making a decision to change both my place and kind of work. And yet, too much of my life has become disconnected from these experiences and cut off from the knowledge they bear of the totality of existence in the universe. My education, like most modern education, has been specialized and fragmented, and I live separated from earth and sky by walls and ceilings, machines, lights, noise, and the press of other people. Even today I look too seldom off my deck at the stars or at the San Francisco skyline. These moments of unity and intensity come to me and to all of us rarely, for in the West we do not as a rule attend to these experiences or give them cultural recognition; our modern professional disciplines have for the most part defined them as anomalous, mystical, irrelevant, or unimportant—an indulgence. They cannot, after all, be tested. Controlled studies to verify them cannot be conducted. They seem to bear no *evidence*.

I would like to argue nevertheless that such experiences, synthesizing as they do the internal and external environments, carry meaning, knowledge, and health. During these timeless moments, there is no barrier between inner and outer space; in fact, time and space melt away and reveal themselves to be the mental constructions they really are. With this harmony come awe and an overwhelming sense of well-being, one that nurtures and heals. The sense of interconnection and relationship that such events carry can be overpowering. Their peace and playfulness evoke visions of the womb and remind us of our wistful imaginings that this was how human life was long ago—timeless, capacious, without boundaries or separation and without the need to control.

What kind of knowledge do these experiences bear? They are certainly not cognitive in the "left-brained," analytic and limited sense in which our modern disciplines have defined knowledge. And yet if health is the ability to respond with our entire being to the environment, to be fully awake, then these experiences are examples of such perfect health, experiences of almost excruciating aliveness. This is their knowledge; it is not cognition but a knowing experienced by all our faculties, not just by the analytic mind. This knowledge goes beyond anything words can express.

It is, however, difficult for many of us to recognize such experiences as bearing knowledge because they are not, to use the modern short-hand that locates thought in the brain, the left-brained, analytic, reductionist, controlled thinking that has evolved into modern science and technology. They include this mode of thought, but they also include the "right brain," with its intuition, its responsiveness, and its dream-like non-linear, diffuse knowledge. Beyond the "right brain" is a much more primitive brain, one that deals with the basic biological functions of the organism and that responds to changes in dilation of the vessels and the production of hormones and messages from the larger nervous systems. In the West, at least since Descartes and probably since long before, we have acted as if the mind were only the left brain, as if, in my father's words, "Nothing exists below the head." We are rewarded professionally and academically for left-brain activity; we have been taught that only such mental work is really serious. And so, although we look at the stars and the moon and "ooh" and "ah," we do not permit ourselves to appreciate the feelings they evoke in us until we can comprehend, cognize, analyze and name the celestial bodies and their connection to us and the world. The spontaneity of complete response to the sky has been denied us by our history, our traditions, and our conventions about what real knowledge is.

Other cultures have responded differently. Many non-Western and spiritual traditions actually train their members for such responsiveness because they recognize it as the integrating and health-giving joy it really is. As these cultures have been broken apart by the forces of modernization, some of their exiled teachers have come among us to share their knowledge and training. In Berkeley, for example, Tarthang Tulku, Rinpoche, an accomplished lama of the Nyingma School of Tibetan Buddhism, has taught and written for many years, notably in a path-breaking study entitled *Time, Space and Knowledge* that sets out to present the teachings of the Tibetan tradition in a form accessible to Westerners. Tarthang Tulku begins this work with a discussion of the sky and progresses through a series of meditation exercises designed to lead the reader to explore inner and outer space, the vast spaces within the reader's "giant body" and the great empty spaces of the universe. In one exercise, to be performed on a mountain top or a high hill, Tarthang Tulku directs the reader to breathe in the blue sky and breathe it out, so that there is complete commingling, so that one finds space "is literally a food that you are eating or grazing on." This and the other exercises in this book are to be undertaken without goals, achievement-orientation, or a sense of direction. They offer nourishment, harmony, and the experience of spaciousness, freedom, and choice. Tarthang Tulku teaches that opening to space brings health; it loosens the sense of density, pressure, rush, and crowding that spoils our days. The book also offers exercises that play in a similar way with time and with knowledge.

These and related teachings seem to harken back to our earliest human roots. I suspect that they may be remnants of great spiritual traditions that once informed cultures in many parts of the world, perhaps even here as well among Native Americans. Anthropologists have reported tracings of such teachings in many parts of the globe. The Dogon of the French-speaking Sudan, for example, have a belief system that interrelates humans, family, village, fields, mountains, and sky. They see each one as an organism, part of a larger organism and connected by subtle forces into a cosmological myth of the totality of the universe. This tribe has a concept of "living interrelated systems," that are always in flux, an ecological vision as sophisticated as any devised by modern science.

If the West ever had a knowledge of interrelationship and connection, how did we lose it? It seems that we have slowly, unrelentingly oppressed ourselves by the nature of the environment we have created for ourselves. What vision of control and struggle has caused us to straighten our floors and walls and to try to straighten even our rivers so that our water will flow in straight lines? When and how did we lose our ability to interact subtly with the universal, curving rhythms that connect us to the sky, to stars, to water, air, and space? Our science of medicine is no longer a discipline of healing; most of our physicians see themselves as medical technicians who combat disease, control the body, and have no special knowledge of the rhythms of life and death. Our social scientists, our public planners, and our politicians operate with similar models of separation, manipulation, and control.

And the costs to us of separation, manipulation, and control are high, for we are robbed of our senses and our very health. We engineer our crops, pouring vast amounts of chemical fertilizers onto our fields so that the water table is slowly, inexorably poisoned, while isolated and healthy tribesmen in New Guinea, who reportedly have no nitrogen in their diet, seem to breathe it in from the air. It has been reported that these tribesmen have a tremendous amount of nitrogen in their stool, and some scientists speculate that through their breath the nitrogen is absorbed and turned by bacterial flora into protein, as the bacteria interact with carbohydrates. Thus, these tribesmen have the protein and nitrogen they need to grow. This is truly "grazing on space." Meanwhile in the West, as we have retreated to our controlling left brain, we have literally lost our senses. As Rene Dubos has written, when a sense dies, when, for example, we no longer hear or smell in our noisy, stinking cities, we become disconnected and dis-eased. Assaulted as we are by chemical vapors and separated by smoke and smog from the air, we breathe shallowly and without awareness. But breath, as the New Guinea tribesmen know and many religions teach, is the very source of being. Breath is *prana,* the energy of life.

Every age invents the past it needs, often as a dream of healing, an Eden where the urgent wrongs of our time did not exist, and rupture and separation had not yet taken place. Thus as an alienated Westerner, I imagine that long ago and before language, humans existed as part of a whole where the trees and fields, the weather, the rocks, the mountains and the sky were all unified and harmonious. Humans lived in this environment as if there were no boundaries, or as if apparent boundaries were osmotic. Inside and outside could hardly be determined. The resources were there. They changed with the rhythm of the seasons, giving clues that were sensed and responded by unconscious mechanisms.

In compressing them, it seems as if humans, arising out of the cradle of Eastern Africa, took two pathways: those who lived in and faced a hostile environment, and those who lived in the warmer more hospitable climate where they could exist more freely with the environment.

A hostile environment provokes in humans a response even as it does in rat colonies. Innovation in these colonies occurs only in the strongest of the have-not rats. Without thinking, somehow they can create and innovate. The haves hold onto the status quo. The remainder of have nots remain oppressed and unable to get what they need. This pattern among rats may give a clue to how humans begin to cope, deal, learn how to live with, and ultimately control a hostile environment.

The earliest means used to deal with the hostile environment clearly changed it little. Yet these means—fire and tools—began the developmental path of skill production to protect the human organism with food, clothing and shelter. Aerial photographs taken today reveal ancient remnants of patterns of nomadic tribes traveling with the wind and seasons and the climate. The rhythms of life slowly began to settle down into closed compounds, villages and houses. It was this beginning and the revolution in the creation of agriculture and the storage of food that began to create another way of being for humans.

Slowly there evolved a more serious need, one previously not required: to communicate and respond verbally. Rather than communicating with minimum words as in their previous existence, they created language. Techniques of science and education geared to creating people who would fit the need to control the environment— the collecting and storing of food, the putting up of walls and roofs over and around their bodies, and the creation of means of preventing others from taking their goods—slowly emerged. This language, one of the keys to behavior control, changed the natural environment.

They squared the fields, straightened the rivers, flattened the mountains, and blocked the sky. Control meant fragmentation, disconnectedness, and separation. The need to control changed consciousness. Ever more precise, words replaced the multivalent symbols and images that had evoked the totality of existence. Words created a magic of their own, and as they became combined as language, they created a structure around which a way of being evolved.

In shorthand, let me call this creation by our ancestors who faced the hostile environments a way of left-brain thinking. Left-brained as we are—measuring, counting, analyzing, becoming more and more cognitive—we still retain another part and need to connect to it. The awe of the jeweled night, the reverence for the baby turtles at dawn, come through spontaneously on occasion, especially as children explore what surrounds them. Many of us carry secrets of ecstatic experience which came at moments when we sensed our connectedness to all that exists, moments that affect our lives and well-being and yet are not part of the daily accepted life of our rational, cognitive, analytic world. Language fails us. Words somehow never express such experience. The natural circadian rhythms that are in all beings have gradually gotten out of synchrony with the rhythms of the total environment, including the sky. Where the moon, sun and stars were once related to all behavior, as in astrology or geomancy, they are now lost, as they are too often for me.

These moments and the subtle interaction with the universal rhythms that connect us are no longer clearly understood by most Westerners, for complex multiple reasons in our long and unique history. But even as we spread our model of development around the world, even as we teach other cultures to tamper with the ebb and flow of existence, to change the earth's flora and substitute twenty or so "productive" plants for the *sixty thousand* once consumed by man, many sensitive spirits in the West recognize that we have reached the limits of manipulation. The control model no longer works. Presidents, corporations, schools, universities, and even families have found that they have to search for other solutions, other ways to live and to deal with the environment. "Go with the flow" is part of the pop culture. Sophisticated scientists have begun to see that living systems are not static and controlled but are inquiring and grow and learn. As we begin to understand social learning, we slowly discover delicate ecological relationships. We find again the work of pioneering nineteenth-century scientists such as Haeckel who taught about interconnection in ways that speak directly to the modern ecology movement. About interconnectedness we begin to wonder, with Rudolph Steiner, how the rhythms of the sky affect plants, animals, and human beings.

For in so controlling the environment, by putting up walls and roofs and floors, by damming the rivers, flattening mountains, and furrowing fields in straight lines, we have created a world that runs counter to nature's wave-like rhythmical energies. Where the Chinese, for whom nature has been beneficent, still recognize the power of force lines in the earth—what we might call biomagnetic fields—we have acted and built as if these do not exist. Westerners may once have possessed this knowledge, for there is evidence that the cathedrals, healing centers, and hospitals of Europe, notably England, may have been built along these lines of energy. Early hospitals could not and did not separate healing from the spiritual energy that they found in the earth. From the Chinese, we learn also about rhythms of energy within the body, about the meridians in acupuncture and the idea that when energy is blocked and does not flow along these channels, disease results. Treatment according to such principles is healing; it means re-establishing harmony and flow, allowing the natural rhythms their expression. It is not, as in the Western model, the *engineering* of "health."

The signs of the Western rediscovery of health as the integration of inner and outer space are everywhere, from the growth of new religions such as Subud, where energy is the focus, to the work of the Peckham Health Center in London, where they have discovered that health is the synthesis of the internal and external environments, to the work of modern physicists and astronomers, who speak almost mystically of a holographic universe where each part contains within it the reflections of the whole. It is to the work of these physical scientists that I wish to turn now, for they seem to unify the disparate strands of human knowledge, control versus non-control, East versus West. Modern physicists, after generations of analytic Western scientific thought, speak in language that could have come out of mystical vision, from Carlos Castaneda's Don Juan, from Taoism, from the Dogon, or from Kalahari world of myth. There are many paths to knowledge.

Geoffrey Chew, a professor of physics at Berkeley, notes that modern physics, having moved from a mechanistic, Newtonian view of the universe to quantum theory, became preoccupied with the innumerable particles that make up the atom. Chew has suggested that if we continue to search, we will find endless particles in the atom. There may in fact be innumerable worlds in both infinities, for the recent report that we have discovered two distant galaxies may mean that we will also continue to find endless new worlds in the stars.

Chew goes on to suggest, in his Bootstrap Theory, that no piece or part can be separated from any other, whether in the sub-atomic world or in the most distant galaxies. The inner universe, unlike the stars, is not made up of particles that are things, but rather of waves and energy that take different forms, depending on how we perceive them. Chew suggests that all the pieces and parts are related to each other and that their relationship includes the presence of the participant-observer who, by virtue of his own consciousness, determines the rest of existence. To put it simply, the consciousness of the observer determines what kind of reality is observed and what kinds of laws exist in the realms of physics. The observer cannot be separated from the observed. The so-called space between particles is not space at all, because the particles are part of that energy field, and that energy field is affected by and related to the consciousness of the observer. My clear implication is that time and space, as Einstein pointed out, are relative and have no objective existence, because they have been brought to perception by the participant-observer.

Another prominent physicist, David Bohm, has described the universe as a hologram in which the whole exists in each of its parts, so that to travel from here to there may not require a journey through "space." The world of the physicists and the world of the Tibetan lamas move closer together; the inner and outer sky may be the last two frontiers. For within the atoms that make us up are vast spaces and bundles of energy, whirling around in a vast universe that resembles nothing so much as the sky. The processes that are at work slowly generate the structures we see, the particles, waves, manifestations of patterns, and relationships. We cannot see energy.

Even our own body cells may be holographic. The Stanford neurophysiologist Karl Pribram, working in cooperation with David Bohm, has suggested that the brain may operate holographically, that each cell may contain within it all memories, recorded in mandala form. Data may be present there in shadowy form, but it seems that it is our own programming that creates a commonly agreed-upon reality. The brain may be like a hologram, then, perceiving a holographic universe.

There is more recent scientific work that discloses the vastness and complexity of our inner universe. Each cell in humans is not just a cell with its own DNA molecules, but a collection of interacting pieces. Each was once a former cell that was really different, and altogether they make up a complex cell or a whole that is greater than anything that the pieces suggest. A vast mixture of DNA exists within a larger environmental context that helps create the whole. Complex cells with other complex cells create each of us, a vast whole of which we are hardly conscious, and yet one that has begun to become self-organizing. This vast mixture of DNA exists within a larger environmental context that helps create its whole not unlike the Dogon vision of organisms within organisms. The vast whole that we barely know is created not only by itself or by its DNA but in large part by the environment of which it is a part.

The environment that has shaped and narrowed the potential offered each of us by our DNA also conforms us to the very environment we have created and leaves unexpressed much of what we might be if we had used ourselves and our environment in a different manner. We are aware more and more, through the knowledge we remember or borrowed from the East and the so-called "primitives," that there are other ways of being, other realities that exist parallel to our own which we cannot see or touch because we have been programmed in other ways. The lessons of Lynn Andrews in *Jaguar Women and the Wisdom of the Butterfly* and others are clues that other planes of reality exist. These realities are no longer just in the realm of science fiction.

To tie these theories to Pribram's holographic brain, it is possible to suggest that in fact the tremendous diversity of DNA in our cells is such that we may have within this DNA the capability of reaching memories and experiences that may not be our own, but that we cannot do so, or cannot easily do so, because our programming, education, and choice of a particular reality prevent us.

Still, I remember vividly as a child imagining riding on a planet of electrons in a solar system as a part of a larger universe that somehow existed inside me. What was this experience? And what of Olaf Stapledon's experience, reported in the *Starmaker,* when he lay on an English lawn and found himself traveling from place to place in all the universes throughout the sky, exploring civilizations at different states of development with different patterns and different creations? Was this a report of the inner experience of the stars or a journey into outer space, travelling many years in advance of our spacemen? It was a holographic experience, finding within one's being the totality of existence.

Most of us have closed our senses to the breadth of the universe, focusing on day-by-day existence. We have found that in doing so we have created pathology and a sense of disconnection. The sky for so long in human history gave us an orientation. We used it to find out where we were. It located us as a part of space, and in so doing, allowed us to be alive, vibrant, and energetic. We have learned that people disconnected from other people are more subject to illness and death than those who are connected. The isolated get sick, face more crises, and heal less well. Isolation from the universe, inner and outer, may produce similar pathology.

As I wrote this, I found myself staring out the window. There were busy streets and cars and noise, but I found myself centering on a pine tree some fifty yards away. I looked at the needles of the branch and found myself unable to tear myself away. It is almost as if, for those moments, and they were fleeting, I was connected not just to the tree and to the earth, but to the whole sky that it pointed up towards. I turned back, refreshed, to my writing, and was able to go on.

My health is not the disease I do not have, nor is it my brain functioning to do the tasks of work or thinking. It is all my being, seeing the tree, the other side of the tree, and its connection to the universe. Looking at the tree, removing the noises of the human-made day, is somehow like giving up for a moment my adult state and becoming a child who can feel wonder at the simplest things. It is easy to get caught up in the words of my professional, medical, adult life because those words create reality. But these words leave out the images, the visions, and the sensations of outer space which connect me, not to medicine, but to health.

Indeed some of the new healing techniques include guided imageries and the places that people go for healing are the natural environments in their minds, or even to visions of flying through space. It is the shaman of the primitive tribe who has somehow been able to couple both the right and the left brain. Not only do shamans—modern and ancient—cure by whatever science they have, but they create a healing process through rituals, music, and dance, in connection with the world around including the stars. Modern medicine has treated well, but heals poorly. It leaves us disconnected in our fragmented hospitals, clinics, and doctors' offices. And so people are recommending Outward Bound, mountain and sea adventures and other outside activity that connects us to the environment, as healing methods for the ill and for those of us who just get tired.

Connectedness, knowing where one is by looking at the stars, creates a pattern by which we proceed. That is health. In the beginning, the Zohar states, there was energy, everything and nothing, no time, no space, no knowledge, no thought. Suddenly a pattern emerged. Something fell into place. Out of the amorphousness, order was created—a pattern. From the light, out of energy, came the letters, the male, the female, and the pillar that held them together, the Tree of Life. And as all these letters-numbers emerged, they reassembled into a new pattern; the name of God and humans were created together.

A myth perhaps, a mystical story, shared with the astronomers, for the fertilization of the cosmic egg, the big bang theory of Fred Hoyle, or the Zohar, shared by the myths of creation, have many commonalities. We do know that the universe is self-organizing. All life goes beyond self-maintenance, becomes transcended into consciousness. The limit of our consciousness is that which we choose and that which causes us difficulty. It is that limiting, the non-use of our various available consciousnesses, that may make us ill.

It is said in Dogon mythology that the origins of life were in the heavens, and especially in the star Sirius B, one they knew existed long before the astronomers discovered it. They knew Sirius B as a heavy, dark mass from which came earth's life. Fred Hoyle has even suggested that from these heavens come meteors, and with them viruses—primitive forms of DNA molecules. These foreign-space molecules entered our mass of nothingness and everything, and shaped the patterns of the simplest of chemicals that are stirred into the beginnings of life, DNA, new DNA, and more over time until humans emerged. Out of the massive disorganization came pattern and light, the viruses, the cells, the DNA building blocks of the tree of life. His theories parallel the Dogon myth that life came from the heavens.

I tie this all together for we "thank Heaven" from where life has come. The tales of the Dogon are similar to those of the Egyptian tales of Osiris and Isis. In our myths are our unconscious memories of the beginnings. They are fuzzy, ghostly, amorphous, and unclear. They require intuition, piecing together—pieces and parts—to find a pattern that exists but that we have not seen. Out failure at control has reawakened this memory. This memory ties us together with the universe. This synthesis of the internal and external, our environs, is health.

Appendix II

Annotated Bibliography on Healthy Cities

Prepared by Dr. Trevor Hancock, York University, Toronto

BERRY, BRIAN J. and KASARDA, JOHN D. (1977). *Contemporary Urban Ecology*. New York, Macmillan Publishing Company.

Aimed at graduate level classes, this book is written from the perspective of urban geography and social ecology. After an introduction, the sections of the book are organized into successive levels of sociospatial hierarchy from neighborhood to total society, looking at the issues at each level from a variety of perspectives from social behaviour through to planned societal change. The authors consider that the contemporary ecological approach is concerned with interdependence, is macrosocial in its perspective, concerned with social system growth and development and is evolutionary in its perspective.

CARLISLE, NORMAN and CARLISLE, MADELYN (1980). *Where to Live for Your Health*. New York, Harcourt Brace Jovanovich.

Like Shakman's books, this one is focussed upon the physical environment, and within that almost entirely on climate and air quality. Chapters discuss atmospheric pressure, heat and cold, humidity, sunlight, air ions, altitude, air and water pollution and noise. A necessary but not sufficient examination of the topic of where to live for your health.

CLAY, GRADY (1980). *Close-up: How to Read the American City*. Chicago, The University of Chicago Press.

CLEGG, E.J. and GARLICK, J.P. (Eds). *Disease & Urbanization.* London, Taylor and Francis Ltd., 1980.

The focus of this collection of articles is on the ecology of disease. Half of the articles are concerned with issues relevant to the developing world (communicable diseases, nutrition and water quality) and half are related to diseases relevant to the developed world. The latter include an article by Harrison on urbanization and stress including that "city residents in the developed world are at greater 'risk' from stress, but on the objective scales, at least, this is not a dramatic phenomenon" as well as articles on chronic lung disease, cancer and coronary heart disease.

DOXIADIS, CONSTANTINE (1974). *Anthropopolis: A City for Human Development.* Athens, Centre of Ekistics.

In this book, Doxiadis, founder of the "science" of ekistics, proposes that the goal of the city is "to make the citizens happy and safe and help them in their human development." He defines five principles that describe human needs with respect to the city (including maximizing contact, minimizing effort, optimizing protective space) five things that anthropos (man) demands in his city (freedom and ability to move, safety, quality of life, human contacts, creativity) and looks at the specifications for the city on a lifecycle basis. His ideal city ends up looking remarkably like a Greek global village! Provocative stuff, if you can stand the neologisms.

DOXIADIS, CONSTANTINE (1977). *Ecology & Ekistics.* Boulder, CO, Westview Press.

This short book, edited after Doxiadis's death in 1975 by Gerald Dix, tries to relate ecology to ekistics. In many ways it is a summation of Doxiadis's work, presenting a sophisticated and enormously complex model of the human environment as seen by Doxiadis, what he calls "the anthropocosmos model." In essence, Doxiadis proposes using a taxonomy of human settlements akin to that of Linnaeus's classification of the plant and animal kingdoms. An overview of the model is presented.

DUHL, LEONARD J. (Ed). *The Urban Condition: People and Policy in the Metropolis.* New York, Clarion Books, 1963.

A collection of articles on a wide range of topics on the broad theme of urbanization and mental health. The articles are in five main sections: man and his environment; renewal and relocation; social action—and reaction; strategies of intervention; and the ecology of the social environment. Contributions come from psychologists, sociologists, urban planners, public health physicians, the legal profession and others.

FORGAYS, DONALD G. (Ed) (1978). *Primary Prevention of Psychopathology Volume 2: Environmental Influences.* Hanover, N.H., University Press of New England.

GREER, ANN L. and GREER, SCOTT (Eds). *Cities & Sickness: Health Care in Urban America* (Urban Affairs Annual Reviews, Vol. 25). Beverly Hills, Sage Publications, 1983.

This volume is almost entirely about the health care system in American cities. There is, however, a section on urbanization and health status which suggests that urban health status is at least as good as rural health status today, perhaps better. There is also an extensive article by McKinlay, et al., showing the comparative unimportance of health care services in improving health in modern day America.

HALL, ELLEN. *Inner City Health in America*. Washington, D.C., Urban Environmental Foundation, 1979.

This brief report examines some of the social and environmental factors that make the inner city an unhealthy place for its inhabitants. The report is a call to action, and urges the development of coalitions among environmentalists, health workers, social justice and civil rights groups and the labor movement to organize to change the conditions.

HEALTH PROGRAMS BRANCH, HEALTH & WELFARE CANADA (1976). *Health Promotion through Designed Environment: Conference Report.* Ottawa, Health & Welfare Canada.

The report of the conference with contributions from Ivan Illich, Leonard Duhl, Kiyo Izumi and Hans Selye. The conference organizers conclude that "the built environment must offer opportunities for self reliance in matters of health."

HINKLE, LAWRENCE E. and LORING, WILLIAM C. (Eds). *The Effect of the Manmade Environment on Health and Behavior.* Atlanta, Center for Disease Control, U.S. Public Health Service, 1977 (DHEW Publication No. (CDC) 77-8318).

The papers published in this book represent an endeavor by the Public Health Service to gain a better understanding of the factors in the residential environment which may offer alternative points for intervention to gain reduction of disease and injury. The focus is upon our current state of knowledge, the need for additional research, the areas for such research and research strategies to be followed. John Cassel's article on "The Relation of the Urban Environment to Health: Toward a Conceptual Frame and a Research Strategy" is particularly valuable. He suggests that once shelter has progressed beyond a basic level, it is the social environment that is the major determinant of health, in particular relationships to other members of the social group and the strength of primary group supports. In a final section, Hinkle suggests that all of the authors "have agreed that the physical variables of the manmade environment affect human health and behavior primarily as they are modified and mediated by the social and psychological characteristics of the people who use the environment."

JACOBS, ALLAN B. *Looking at Cities*. Cambridge, MA, Harvard University Press, 1985.

This book, by an urban planner, is about how we look at the city. Believing that "the more conscious we are of the relationship between what is observed and what actions are taken, the more likely we are to have better, more humane, more livable cities." Jacobs describes in some detail how we should look at the city—its buildings, land and landscape, artifacts, commercial areas, street patterns, the public environment, changes in the city and the city's people. There are innumerable clues for us, and Jacobs believes that "the whole process of looking, questioning, trying to gain understanding, makes a person a more intimate, respectful part of any environment and therefore more likely to be caring of it. That is the basis for good planning and beneficial action."

JACOBS, JANE. *Cities & and the Wealth of Nations: Principles of Economic Life*. New York, Vintage Books, 1985.

In her latest book, this thoughtful and provocative writer on the city argues that it is cities, not nations, that are the vital force in economics. By replacing imports in a ferment of innovation and creativity, cities unleash five forms of growth that are at the root of all economic expansion: "abruptly enlarged city markets for new and different imports consisting largely of rural goods and of innovations being produced in other cities; abruptly increased numbers and kinds of jobs in the import-replacing city; increased transplants of city work into non-urban locations as older enterprises are crowded out; new uses for technology, particularly to increase rural production and productivity; and growth of city capital." She concludes with "a hard plain truth. Societies and civilizations in which the cities stagnate don't develop and flourish further. They deteriorate."

JOFFE, JUSTIN M., ALBEE, GEORGE W. and KELLY, LINDA D. (Eds). *Readings in Primary Prevention of Psychopathology: Basic Concepts*. Hanover, N.H., University Press of New England, 1984.

This collection of readings focuses upon factors that may harm mental health (organic factors, stress and exploitation) and factors that may be important in protecting and enhancing mental health (competence, coping skills, self-esteem and support systems). It is concluded that prevention of psychopathology is possible, but that the biggest problem is powerlessness. While not specifically on urban issues and health, the implications for urban policies are clear.

LEAVITT, JUDITH W. *The Healthiest City: Milwaukee and the Politics of Health Reform*. Princeton, N.J., Princeton University Press, 1982.

This book reviews the history of Milwaukee, its health and its health department, focussing particularly upon the late nineteenth and early twentieth centuries, culminating in the city's consistent high placing in the national health conservation contests of the 1930s.

LINDHEIM, ROSLYN and SYME, S. LEONARD. Environments, People & Health. *Annual Review of Public Health* 1983. 4:335–59.

The authors review the evidence linking social and spatial conditions to health and disease. There is strong evidence that supportive social relationships are important to health, and these can be affected by urban planning and design. Position in the hierarchical status affects health through poor living and working conditions, stigmatization and low self-esteem, and lack of participation and control. They also suggest that a sense of "connectedness" to our biological and cultural heritage is of importance. The implications for urban policy and planning are discussed.

LYNCH, KEVIN. *A Theory of Good City Form*. Cambridge, Massachusetts, MIT Press, 1981.

Kevin Lynch was a respected urban designer and theorist. In this book he lays out his general statement about "the good settlement," restricting himself to the connection between human values and the spatial, physical city. After reviewing several models and theories of the city, he settles upon the concept of the city as an organism/ecosystem. He proposes five dimensions of good city form-vitality (the settlement can be clearly perceived and mentally differentiated in time and space); fit (how well a settlement's spatial patterns match the customary behavior of its inhabitants); access (the ability to reach other persons, activities resources, services, information or places); and control (the degree to which the use and access to space and activities is controlled by those who use, work or reside there). For each dimension, Lynch defines a number of performance characteristics.

MICHELSON, WILLIAM (1976). *Man & his Urban Environment: A Sociological Approach*. Reading, MA, Addison-Wesley Publishing Co.

Michelson examines the urban environment in relation to five key sociological variables: lifestyle, lifecycle, social class, values and psychosocial pathology. Michelson examines the extent to which the urban physical environment determines behavior and social interaction, and the role of social science in improving urban design.

MICHELSON, WILLIAM, LEVINE, SAUL V. and MICHELSON, ELLEN (1979). *The Child in the City: Today and Tomorrow*. Toronto, University of Toronto Press.

This is the first of two volumes resulting from "The Child in the City Program". This volume contains a collection of papers by sociologists, urban planners, psychologists, public health and medical practitioners, and others originally presented as a lecture series. The volume concludes by outlining some key issues for the family, the social structure and the physical setting, and outlines five major themes that are explored in the second volume: community services, childrearing systems, children and the law, ethnic diversity, the urban physical environment.

MICHELSON, WILLIAM, LEVINE, SAUL V. and SPINA, ANNA-ROSE (1979). *The Child in the City: Changes and Challenges.* Toronto, University of Toronto Press.

In this second volume of the "Child in the City Program" the themes identified in volume 1—children, families and community services; child-rearing systems and the influence of shared childrearing on the development of competence; children and the law; issues for adolescence; ethnic diversity and children; children and the urban physical environment; are explored in greater detail. A concluding chapter outlines some emergent themes— competence, (the child's ability to cope with, adapt to and control the environment in which she lives; the rights of children and the responsibilities we can reasonably expect of them; the accountability of social institutions to the individual; the interconnectedness of all the effects upon children and the environmental mosaic within which they live; and finally the effect of poverty on the child.

MOORE, et al. (1980). *The Biocultural Basis of Health: Expanding Views of Medical Anthropology.* St. Louis, Mosby.

This is an examination of health and human behavior from the perspective of medical anthropology. Three major themes are explored, namely human adaptation, the lifecycle as it relates to health, and the cultural belief system as it relates to health. Health is "seen to result from adaptation and sickness from the failure of adaptation to occur. Both biological and cultural factors are integral to this evolutionary process." The authors call for health care policies that take cultural influences into account, with the emphasis upon the life cycle, humanistic health care and the significance of human scale.

MORRIS, DAVID (1982). *Self Reliant Cities: Energy and the Transformation of Urban America.* San Francisco, Sierra Club Books.

In this book David Morris, President of the Institute for Local Self-Reliance, looks at urban energy use and its impact upon the city. He looks at the way that energy has shaped the American city, examines the impact of the energy crisis upon the city and proposes that the global energy crisis can be solved by local action, in particular the development of "the ecological city". The concluding chapter shows how cities can become more self reliant in terms of energy and raw materials using the fruits of modern technology.

MORRIS, DAVID (1982). *The New City States*. Washington, D.C., Institute for Local Self-Reliance.

The President of this institute suggests that "the city is becoming an ecological nation". He suggests that the city has never been viewed as a producer of basic wealth (but see Jane Jacobs, 1984), but points to a variety of ways in which the city can generate its own wealth. He proposes a marriage of decentralization and local democracy with modern technology and human scale production systems.

MUMFORD, LEWIS (1938). *The Culture of Cities*. New York, Harcourt, Brace & Co.

MUMFORD, LEWIS (1961). *The City in History: Its Origins, Its Transformations and Its Prospects*. New York, Harcourt, Brace & World.

MUMFORD, LEWIS (1968). *The Urban Prospect*. New York, Harcourt, Brace & World.

PAINE, LESLIE H. (Ed). *Health Care in Big Cities*. New York, St. Martin's Press, 1978.

This is a collection of papers and reports prepared for an International Hospital Federation congress in Tokyo in 1977. The health services of eleven large cities from all over the world are described, as well as particular aspects of services such as mental health, regionalization, policy and planning. In spite of the comment in the introduction (by Miles Hardie) that "political, social and economic change will often have far greater effect in improving standards than changes in the organization and management of health services," the overwhelming emphasis of each report is on health (sick) care services.

PHILLIPS, E. BARBARA and LeGATES, RICHARD. *City Lights: An Introduction to Urban Studies*. New York, Oxford University Press, 1981.

This is a comprehensive and very useful introduction to urban studies. The authors begin with an assumption that what you see depends on how you look at it, that things urban are best understood in a broad context from an interdisciplinary perspective and that social action cannot be separated from social theory. After a section on different ways of looking at and thinking about the city, they trace the development of cities and of urban theories, examine different concepts of "community," look at structures, hierarchies and power; examine urban planning, urban design and urban form; and conclude by looking at the economics of production and consumption, work, poverty and fiscal policy.

SHAKMAN, ROBERT A. (1981). *Where You Live may be Hazardous to Your Health: A Health Index to over 200 American Communities.*

In this book, Shakman reviews the cities primarily from a geographical perspective. Issues such as altitude and topography, climate, natural disasters, allergy and air pollution are discussed, and in addition a section on crime is included in each profile. There is however, no discussion of the sociological dimensions of health, with the minor exception of crime. As a result, the book is seriously flawed.

WEINSTEIN, MALCOLM (1980), *Health in the City: Environmental & Behavioural Influences.* New York, Pergamon Press.

References

Andrews, Lynn. *Jaguar Women and the Wisdom of the Butterfly Tree*. New York: Harper and Row, 1985.

Ariyaratne, A.T. *Collected Works*. Colombo, 1983.

Barry, Wendell. "Poetry and Marriage". San Francisco: This was quoted in a brochure from the Jung Institute. (I have no idea where they got it, it is a nice quotation.)

Bateson, Gregory. *Mind and Nature*. New York: Bantam Books, 1980.

Bennett, J.G. *The Dramatic Universe*, Vol, IV. Sherbourne, England: Coombe Springs Press, 1966.

Benton, Itzhak. *Stalking the Wild Pendulum*. New York: Bantam Books, 1979.

Berkowitz, Bill. *Community Dreams: Ideas for Enriching Neighborhood and Community Life*. San Luis Obispo, CA: Impact Publishers, 1984.

Berry, Brian J. and Kasarda, John D. *Contemporary Urban Ecology*. New York: McMillian, 1977.

Blair, Lawrence. *Rhythms of Vision*. New York: Schocken, 1976.

Bly, Robert. *News of the Universe*. San Francisco: Sierra Club, 1980.

Bohm, David. *Revision Journal*, Vol. 1, No. 3–4, Summer-Fall 1978.

Bowen, Elizabeth. *Return to Laughter*.

Boyatzis, Richard. *The Competent Manager: A Model for Effective Performance*. New York: Wiley, 1982.

Brecher, Kenneth and Feirtag, Michael (Eds). *Astronomy of the Ancients*. Cambridge: MIT Press, 1980.

Brecht, Bertolt. *Three Penny Opera*.

Burr, Donald. Tarrytown Letter. Tarrytown, August 1984.

Burr, Saxton. *Blueprint for Immortality: The Electric Patterns of Life.* London: Neville Spearman, 1977.

Campbell, Joseph. *Mythic Image.* Princeton: Princeton University Press, 1974.

Capra, Fritjof. *The Tao of Physics.* Berkeley: Shambhala Books, 1975.

Capra, Fritjof. *The Turning Point: Science, Society and Rising Culture.* New York: Simon & Schuster, 1982.

Cesaire, Aime. *Pan Africanism* as quoted by Colin Legum. London: Pall Mall Press, 1962.

Chew, Geoffrey, Cell, Mann and Rosenfeld, Arthur. Strongly attracting particles. *Scientific American,* Vol. 210, pp. 74–83, Fall 1964.

Community Era Task Force. *At the Crossroads.* Spokane, WA: Community Era Task Force, 1984.

de Saint Exupery. *Wind, Sand and Stars.* New York: Harcourt, Brace, Jovanovich, Inc., 1967.

deChardin, Teilhard. *Man's Place in Nature.* New York: Harper & Row, 1966.

Douglas, Mary. *Purity and Danger: An Analysis of Concepts of Pollution and Taboo.* London: Routledge & Kegan Paul, 1966.

Doxiadis, Constantine. *Ecology and Ekistics.* Boulder, CO: Westview Press, 1977.

Drury, Nevill. *The Path of the Chameleon, Encounter with the Gods and Magic.* St. Helier, England: Spearman, 1973.

Dubos, Rene. *Mirage of Health.* New York: Harper & Row, 1979.

Duhl, Leonard. *Health Planning and Social Change.* New York: Human Sciences Press, 1986.

Duhl, Leonard J. Health, whole, holy, healing. *Gesar Magazine,* pp. 14–16, Spring 1976.

Duhl, Leonard J. The promotion and maintenance of health: Myth and reality. *Health Promotion Through Designed Environment.* Ottawa, Canada: Ministry of Health, October 1976.

Duhl, Leonard J. The Dimensions of Health or Health for a New Epoch: Traditional Healing and "Modern" Medicine. Paper presented at the Conference on Traditional Medicine, Association of American Indian Physicians, Albuquerque, NM, August 1–2, 1980.

Duhl, Leonard J. The promotion and maintenance of health: Myth and reality. *Health Promotion Through Designed Environment.* Ottawa, Canada: Ministry of Health, October 1976.

Eisley, Lauren. *The Star Thrower.* New York: Harvest, 1979.

Ferris, Timothy. *Galaxies.* San Francisco: Sierra Club, 1980.

Gabriel, Medard. Planning diseases. *The Futurist,* Oct. 1984.

Goleman, Daniel. Scientists find a city is a series of varying perceptions. *New York Times,* pp. 11 & 14, December 31, 1985.

Gorman, Peter. *Pythagoras.* Boston: Routledge & Kegan, 1978.

Graves, Tom and Hoult, Janet (eds). *Essential T.C. Lethbridge.* New York: Routledge & Kegan, 1978.

Graves, Richard. *White Goddess.* New York: Octagon Books, 1972.

Greening, T. *J. Humanistic Pyschology,* Vol. 15, No. 4, p. 91, Fall 1975.

Greer, Scott. Health care in American cities: Dedicated workers in an undedicated system in Greer, Ann L. and Greer, Scott (Eds). *Cities and Sickness: Health Care in Urban America.* Beverly Hills: Sage Publications, 1983.

Griaule, Marcel and Dieferfern, Germaine. In Robert Temple's *The Sirius Mystery.* New York: St. Martin's Press, 1978.

Grossinger, Richard. *Planet Medicine.* New York: Anchor Press, 1980.

Grossinger, Richard. *Night Sky.* San Francisco: Sierra Club, 1981.

Halevi, Z'ev ben Shimon. *A Kabbalistic Universe.* New York: Weiser, 1977.

Hawken, Paul, Ogilvy, James and Schwartz, Peter. *Seven Tomorrows: The Potential Crises That Face Humankind—and the Role of Choice in Determining the Future.* New York: Bantam, 1982.

Hinkle, Lawrence E. and Loring, William C. (Eds). *The Effect of the Manmade Environment on Health and Behavior.* Atlanta, GA: U.S. Public Health Service (DHEW Publication # [CDC]77-8318), 1977.

Hoke, Robert. *Potentials.* (Xeroxed document).

Hougan, Jim, *Decadence: Radical Nostalgia, Narcissism and Decline in the Seventies.* New York: Morrow, 1975.

Hoyle, Fred. *Nature of the Universe.* Harper & Row, 1960.

Jacobs, Jane. *Cities and the Wealth of Nations: Principles of Economic Life.* New York: Random House, 1984.

Kennedy, Donald A. Cities and the wealth of nations: Principles of economic life in Hinkle, Lawrence E. and Loring, William C (Eds), *op cit.*

Kennedy, Robert. Xeroxed speech, 1967.

Koestler, Arthur. *The Act of Creation.* New York: Macmillan, 1964.

L'Engle, Madeline. *A Wrinkle in Time.* New York: Farrar, Straus & Giroux, 1963.

L'Engle, Madeline. *A Wind in the Door.* New York: Dell Publishing Co., Inc., 1978.

L'Engle, Madeline. *A Swiftly Tilting Planet.* New York: Dell Publishing Co., Inc., 1978.

Lalonde, Marc. *A New Perspective on the Health of Canadians.* Ottawa: Health and Welfare Canada, 1974.

Landes, David. *The Unbound Prometheus Technological Change and Industrial Development in Western Europe from 1750 to the Present.* Cambridge, MA: Cambridge University Press, 1969.

Lovelock, J.E. Gaia. *New Look at Life on Earth.* New York: Oxford University Press, Inc., 1979.

Lynch, Kevin. *A Theory of Good City Form*. Cambridge, MA: The MIT Press, 1981.

Macy, Joanna. *Dharma and Development: Religion as Resource in the Sarvodaya Self-Help Movement*. West Hartford, CT: Kumarian Press, 1985 (revised edition).

Margen, Sheldon. Personal Communication, 1983.

Marien, Michael. *Future Survey Annual: 1983*. Washington: World Future Society, 1984.

McKnight, John and Kretzmann, John. Community organizing in the 80's: Toward a post-alinsky agenda. *Social Policy*, pp. 15–17, Winter 1984.

Medard, Gabriel. Planning diseases. *The Futurist*, pp. 21, October 1984.

Meier, Richard L. *A Communication Theory of Urban Growth*. Cambridge, MA: The MIT press, 1962.

Miller, Alice. *Thou Shalt Not Be Aware: Society's Betrayal of the Child*, translated by Hildegarde and Hunter Hannum. New York: Farrar, Straus and Giroux, 1984.

Morris, Jan. *From the Cities*. New York: Oxford University Press, 1985.

Murchie, Guy. *Song of the Sky*. Boston: Houghton Mifflin Co., 1954.

Myers, Norman (Ed.). *Gaia: An Atlas of Planet Management*. Garden City, NY: Anchor Books, Anchor Doubleday, 1984.

Naisbitt, John. *Megatrends*. New York: Warner Books, 1982.

Needleman, Jacob. *New Religions*. New York: E.P. Dutton, 1977.

Nilsson, Lennart. *Behold Man*. Boston: Little, Brown & Co., 1974.

Nutrition Reviews, Vol. 23, No. 10, October 1971.

Pacione, Michael (ed). *Urban Problems and Planning in the Developed World*. New York: St. Martins Press, 1981.

Palen, John. *The Urban World*. New York: McGraw, Hill, 1987.

Pearse, Innes. *Quality of Life*. New York: Columbia University Press, 1980.

Pennich, Nigel. *The Ancient Science of Geomancy*. London: Thames & Hudson, 1979.

Pepper, Elizabeth and Wilcox, John. *Magic and Mystical Sites*. New York: Harper & Row, 1977.

Peters, Thomas J. and Waterman, Robert H. Jr. *In Search of Excellence: Lessons from America's Best-Run Companies*. New York: Warner Books, 1982.

Philips, Burton and LeGates, Richard. *City Lights: An Introduction to Urban Studies*. Oxford: Oxford University Press, 1981.

Pribram, Karl. *Revision Journal*, Vol. 1, No. 3–4, Summer-Fall 1978.

Prigogine, Ilya and Stengers, Isabelle. *Order Out of Chaos: Man's New Dialogue With Nature*. Toronto: Bantam Books, 1984.

Rosen, Sidney. *My Voice Will Go With You*. New York: Norton Press, 1982.

Schwenk, Theodor. *Sensitive Chaos*. New York: Schocken Books, Inc., 1976.

Shah, Idries. *The Sufis*. Garden City, NY: Anchor Doubleday, 1971.

Shah, Idries. *Seek After Truth*. San Francisco: Harper & Row, 1982.

Stapledon, Olaf. *Star Maker*. New York: Penguin, 1973.

Steiner, Rudolph. *Anthroposophic Gardening*. Spring Valley, NY: Anthroposophic Press, Inc., 1979.

Times Books. *Atlas of World History*. London: Times Books, 1980.

Tulku, Tarthang. *Time, Space and Knowledge: A New Vision of Reality*. Emeryville, CA: Dharma Publishing, 1977.

Turner, Frederick. Escape from modernism: Technology and the future of the imagination. *Harper's*, pp. 53–54, November 1984.

Turner, Victor. *The Forest of Symbols: Aspects of Ndembu Ritual*. Ithaca, NY: Cornell University Press, 1967.

van der Post, Laurens. *Lost World of Kalahari*. New York: Harcourt, Brace, Jovanovich, Inc., 1977.

Watson, Lyle. *Supra Nature*. New York: Bantam Press, 1973.

Watson, Lyle. *Gifts of Unknown Things*. New York: Bantam Press, 1979.

Watson, Lyle. *Life Tide*. New York: Simon & Schuster, 1979.

Weber, Eugen. History is what historians do. *The New York Times Book Review*, p. 13, July 22, 1984.

Weber, Max. *Economics and Society*. Berkeley, CA: U.S. Press, (1921) 1979.

Williamson, G. Scott and Pearse, Innes. *Science, Synthesis and Sanity*. London: Collings, 1965.

Winston, Jerry. *Colors from the Zohar*. San Francisco: Barah, 1975.

9 780925 776044